WEIRD EDMONTON

The Odd, Quirky and Wonderful People, Places, History and Hauntings

Mark Kozub

BLUE BIKE BOOKS

First printed in 2013 10 9 8 7 6 5 4 3 2 1
Printed in Canada

The Publisher: Blue Bike Books

Website: www.bluebikebooks.com

Library and Archives Canada Cataloguing in Publication

Kozub, Mark, author

Weird Edmonton : the odd, quirky and wonderful people, places, history and hauntings/ Mark Kozub.

ISBN 978-1-926700-43-4 (pbk.)

1. Edmonton (Alta.)—Miscellanea. I. Title.

FC3696.3.K69 2013 971.23'34 C2013-907304-3

Project Director: Nicholle Carrière
Project Editor: Kathy van Denderen
Illustrations: Roger Garcia, Patrick Hénaff, Graham Johnson, Peter Tyler
Photo Credits: Every effort has been made to accurately credit the sources of photographs. Any errors or omissions should be reported directly to the publisher for correction in future editions. Photographs courtesy of Flickr.com: Creative Commons (p. 62, Wilson Hui; p. 119, Ego Ant; p. 159, Cindy Lou Photos; p. 182, Kevin M. Klerks; p. 189, Stella Blu; p. 196, Hobolens); p. 240, Randall Edwards.
Cover Image: Photo of Art Gallery of Alberta - © Brownstock / Alamy; Background - © Photos.com

Produced with the assistance of the Government of Alberta, Alberta Media Fund.

Alberta
Government

We acknowledge the financial support of the Government of Canada through the Canada Book Fund (CBF) for our publishing activities.

Canadian Heritage Patrimoine canadien

PC: 24

Dedication

For Barbara.

Adventures are 500 times more fun with you by my side.

CONTENTS

ACKNOWLEDGEMENTS

Writing a book is not a solo venture. Yes, the writing has to be done by one crazed writer spending long (*very* long) days hunched over the laptop. Before that happens, though, countless hours of research are spent picking the brains of other people. And even before that, what a writer needs is a publisher to say, "Yes." Thanks to Nicholle Carrière of Blue Bike Books for doing just that! *After* the writing is done, it takes an eagle-eyed editor to ensure the book is ready for public consumption. Thanks to Kathy van Denderen for being one of the best I've worked with!

Huge and in fact planet-sized thanks must also go to Barbara North, for all the amazing research into things ranging from the silly to the nifty to the very far-out. I could not have done this book without you. Thanks also for being a great comedian, a great and creative writer, and especially for being my best friend and the one I love.

I also thank all of my friends, fellow writers, and especially my family, for my life journey so far. Thanks to my mother and father for being the ones who brought me here and for being understanding when raising a young son who (a) wanted to be a Martian, and (b) wanted to be a professional writer, which are both pretty much the same thing. Mom, I miss your great big spirit and how you made Christmas and birthdays a big deal.

Thanks also to my big brother Michael and my little sis "Missy" for putting up with me on all those many nights in my adolescence when I was obsessed (yes, *obsessed*) with sitting and clacking at the typewriter. (Thanks to Brit, too, for being a nifty niece and for being too young to remember typewriters.)

Finally, thanks to the Creator of the Universe, for making a cool earth filled with cool creatures that are super fun to write about and utterly magical to encounter face-to-face.

Life on earth is truly miraculous and precious. Sunrise to sundown, I celebrate it all with gratitude.

INTRODUCTION

I remember it well. It was my first day in kindergarten, and I desperately wanted to make a good impression on the other kids. One of our first in-class "assignments" was to form something with Play-Doh, which was cool, since I played with Plasticine all the time at home and figured it was a bit more "mature" than Play-Doh. So, tongue stuck firmly between my teeth, I eagerly went to work creating.

When it was time for all the kids to do a "show and tell" with our doughy creations, I quickly noticed that most of the other students had made balls.

Seriously. Balls.

When it was my turn, I quite proudly—likely, downright *egotistically*—displayed the marvel-of-modern-man I had constructed.

A little girl across from me cocked her head and squinted. "What *is* it?"

I beamed. "A laser gun!"

The little girl's whole face scrunched, and she pointed right at me. "You're *weird,"* she said.

So here it is, all of these years later, and I'm the proud author of another unusual creation. This time it's a book: *Weird Edmonton.* It's an enthusiastic collection of the elements that make life in this city cool, quirky, fun, goofy and sometimes, yes, downright weird.

In hindsight, I was probably destined to write a book like this. I was born and raised in Edmonton, for starters, which covers the "Edmonton" part. As for the "weird" part—despite growing up in a fairly normal family of vegetable farmers—ever since I was a kid obsessed with sci-fi movies, Martians, deep-sea creatures and anything that seemed a million miles away from weeding rows and rows of carrots or cucumbers, I have always been attracted to the weird.

As a kid, I played bass with the family band, which as a general concept is "quirky," not "weird." Then again, you have to consider that we had gigs like the one where our drummer forgot his drumsticks and had to play with cutlery from the kitchen, or the gig where a kid crawled onto the dance floor and bit the ankles of anyone trying to dance (true story!).

As a journalist, I've taken a Pentecostal preacher to a Marilyn Manson concert, taken a feminist to a Promise Keepers men's rally and even spent a day deep in the bowels of the inner city, where I interviewed a man who believed he knew the exact date of the end of the universe but assured me that Edmonton would survive the damnation "because we have a good library" (no word of a lie!).

I've been a beatnik poet, a punk rock musician wearing a suit and tie (now *that's* punk!) and an on-air radio personality endorsing a fad diet that cost me my gall bladder. I've danced with Sufis and meditated with Rosicrucians. I've found my inner "wild man" while facing an adversary during a super-intense men's weekend called the New Warrior Training Adventure. And there are surely more thoroughly fascinating experiences to come.

No matter how rewarding I found each of the above-noted experiences, I learned something profound while working on this book. I discovered that life is far more magical than meets the eye. I've lived in Edmonton most of my life, but I never knew until now half of the incredible people, places and experiences that are in my own backyard.

I have a challenge for you, dear reader. Whether you live in Edmonton or you're just visiting, while you're here, try to explore a little more than you usually do, and you'll see that there's so much to see and do, and so many fascinating people to meet, that you'd have to live a million lifetimes in order to experience it all.

Why not pack as much as you can into the one life you have, right here, right now?

Take this challenge: make a point of really noticing how many weird and wonderful sights, sounds and situations are going on all around you. I'm serious. Do it for just one week, and I swear you'll want to try it one more time, and yet one more, until finally your eyes are fully opened to the wonder of "weird."

Strange Spirits

I've always loved space. In elementary school I even said in my yearbook I wanted to colonize the moon, but I'm willing to miss the moon to hit Mars.

–Christy Foley, Edmonton woman on short-list for The Mars One Project, a one-way trip to Mars slated for 2024

GHASTLY GHOSTS

On the surface, you might think that Edmonton looks like any other average city. Every day, people bustle off to their respective workplaces, where they gather around their respective water coolers and talk about entirely respectable topics—like weather or retirement plans or what was on TV last night.

But there's another side to Edmonton. Start poking your nose where it doesn't belong and you'll hear about haunted houses and apartment buildings, and even haunted candy stores!

What's more, there are paranormal groups that meet on a monthly basis, mystical stones from outer space, people going into past life experiences under hypnosis, and much more.

Think Edmonton is dull? Think again.

Oh, and if you begin to get the distinct and creeping feeling that you're being watched as you read this chapter, it might be true!

Sweet George

Carol's Quality Sweets has been located in Edmonton's trendy, upscale High Street area ever since their Whyte Avenue area store burnt down in 2003. They were on Whyte Avenue for 13 years. Quite early on during those 13 years, something spooky happened, according to Jeannice Logan, the manager.

"My brother and I were working there one evening and suddenly we saw our door open halfway, and we heard a male voice say, 'Do you wanna go in here?' But there was no one there! And it was a heavy door. There was no way the wind could have blown it open," says Logan.

Not long after that, other unusual, unexplained events started happening. "Once when I was there alone, I saw a footstool with steps suddenly flip open. Another time when I was alone in the shop, I heard footsteps in the back of the store."

Above Carol's Quality Sweets was a psychic shop. The psychic had an empty chair designated for…well, the ghost.

This apparition came to be known as "George." And there's an interesting story behind his existence. "Before that building on Whyte Avenue was ours, it was an apartment building. There was a fire there, and George died in it," says Logan.

Visit Carol's Quality Sweets now, and you won't glimpse the supernatural. But you will certainly find some super awesome treats…like Mega Sour Candies from England. These candies are *so* sour that you can't eat more than three of them in a day without burning off your taste buds.

DID YOU KNOW?

The Princess Theatre on Whyte Avenue is reportedly haunted. Legend has it that projectionists in this movie theatre have witnessed a woman "floating around" above the projection booth.

Phantom Footsteps, Burning Building

The Arlington Apartments building downtown used to be on 100 Avenue and 105 Street. It burned down in 2005, but before then, the tenants claimed they heard phantom footsteps and laughter in the hallway. But no one was there.

Apartment residents in the Arlington also *saw* things—supernatural sorts of things, like spectral images of fine ladies sitting and sipping tea. Also witnessed was an elderly couple that would float above the floor and hover into an elevator and disappear.

That particular elevator in the Arlington hadn't been operational for years.

As for the tea-drinking ladies, when the Arlington was first built in 1909 as a stately Edwardian five-storey red brick building, the reception rooms were at the end of the halls. Inside those rooms, women used to host afternoon teas.

Apparently, they kept on doing so for years after their passing!

The Lobotomized Ghost

Before the Edmonton radio station CKUA moved into its new location in the historic Alberta Hotel on 98 Street and Jasper Avenue in October 2012, it was on Jasper Avenue and 105 Street, where people in the control room felt as if they were being "watched." Other employees commented that when they were in the basement of the building, in the record library, they heard a voice.

It was also reported that a floating face was witnessed in the control room.

When the Alberta Paranormal Investigators Society paid a visit to CKUA in the fall of 2009, they interviewed a number of parties and discovered that the radio station was likely haunted by a man named Sam, who had been a caretaker in the building back in the 1950s and died there, from a coronary.

Yet others have said that Sam was rumoured to have had a mysterious past, and that he had even been lobotomized!

Haunted Ladies Room

Feeling "watched" seems to be a key indication that a place is being haunted by some kind of entity. In the late 1990s at a popular downtown restaurant and bar—one that shall remain nameless out of respect for the current owners—a woman left the ladies room feeling unnerved.

She felt as though she was being watched.

When the woman commented on the experience to one of the staff, the waitress explained that the other waitresses had also felt that way when in the ladies room. Sometimes they would even hear voices calling their name.

The area that the building stood on had once been farmland. There was talk that a young farm girl had been murdered on that farmland.

Swimming Pool Spectres

A City of Edmonton swimming pool apparently has some ghostbusters-like activities going on. Again, giving you the exact location would make its management and patrons uncomfortable. But let's put it this way: if you're at a swimming pool on the southeast side of the city and beach balls are being thrown around entirely on their own, you're in the right place. In addition, you might catch a whiff of men's cologne in the mechanical room—when no man is around!

The beach ball incidents are supposedly the product of a little girl ghost named Emily. She has been heard giggling and has even been known to call out to staff members (and, yes, she knows their names).

As for that men's cologne, some people say that the mechanical room is haunted by a ghost named Hank. He manifests in one of two ways: as a men's cologne or a patch of cloudy air.

Communication from Beyond

Ghosts don't often communicate directly with the living. Of course, not all ghosts have an old-fashioned Underwood typewriter upon which to click-clack a message.

Back in the early 1980s, a married couple in the Edmonton area was plagued by constant paranormal activity in their home. The TV would change channels out of the blue (and this was before the days when remote controls were common in households). After a while, other incidents started happening. The couple would hear a sound coming up from the basement.

Someone was typing on the old typewriter they had downstairs.

No one was down there, though. Well, no one they could see. One day, the woman of the household decided to put a piece of paper in that old Underwood, just to see what message their apparition might type.

After the woman went upstairs to talk with her mother on the phone, about going to visit her, she headed back down into the basement. When she checked the Underwood, typed upon the piece of paper was a message.

"Have a pleasant time at your parents' home," it said.

A Nicer Haunting

In 1977, a family moved into the Old Strathcona area, into a house that was originally built in 1912. The family had two young daughters who told their mother about "the nice lady" who came to visit them in one of the bedrooms.

One of the daughters later claimed that the woman in question was someone who used to live in that house long ago—and was *still* living there, only not in bodily form. The "nice lady" would come to her in times when she needed soothing.

In other words, this ghost wasn't there to haunt.

She was there to comfort.

The Firkins House

In Fort Edmonton Park you will find a well-preserved home originally owned by Dr. Ashley M. Firkins, a highly regarded American adventurer and dentist who moved to Edmonton from Chicago in 1912.

Step inside and see if you feel the hair on your arms stand on end.

There's a good chance you will. Some people have claimed to see a woman's spirit floating by a bookcase. Some swear they've witnessed a dummy—a ventriloquist's doll—suddenly appearing in the cupboards. Others have spoken about seeing the ghost of a young boy who is sickly. Still others say the boy is actually a teenager studying a book of magic.

From there, the stories get much, much more fantastical. And creepy.

According to some of the stories, the boy was Dr. Firkins' son. After being padlocked in a storage space, he was murdered. By his father.

In 1992 when Fort Edmonton Park's officials were getting the Firkins house from the family that was presently living in it (the Kareptz family), they were warned that the house was haunted. While the construction crew was repairing the house, strange things started happening. Tools went missing, and windowpanes would fall and land absolutely intact.

As if to thicken the mystery, Dr. Firkins never had a son. He and his wife had two daughters.

A Ghost Story of My Own

In my younger years—1993, to be exact—I got tired of the pathetically puny bachelor suite in which I was living and decided to move in with a roommate to a bigger place. We did the obligatory search for a rental property. When we parked outside a particular house in Edmonton's Oliver area, my first words to my friend were, "Nice, but it looks haunted."

As it turned out, I was right. How else can I explain the strange incidents that happened after we moved in? The first two months were incident free. Then one night my platonic female roommate saw a shadowy figure at the foot of her bed. "Are you a sleepwalker?" she asked me the next day.

"Not to my knowledge," I said.

A week or so later, after returning home from a late-night gig with a band I was playing with at the time, my roommate once again brought up the topic of me being a sleepwalker. "Are you sure that shadowy figure wasn't you?" she asked.

I groaned, growing a little impatient with the whole questioning. "I'm not a sleepwalker. What do I have to do to convince you?"

And just then, at that exact moment, we both heard someone walking across the floor upstairs—and heard the floor give a loud *creeeeeeeak.*

When we went to inspect the upstairs, both of us trembling, we didn't find anything.

Not long after that, my brother came over for a video night (and, yes, this was when we had "videos," not DVDs or Netflix). As he was leaving, he had a strange look on his face. He didn't explain it until the next day. Over the phone, he told me that when he had looked up at the top of the stairs he saw, for just a brief moment, a little girl in old-fashioned clothes and with her hair in ringlets.

A week or so later, my roommate and I heard a loud crash upstairs. Again, when we went to inspect, there was no sign that anything unusual had happened.

A few nights after that, I had a dream that someone was at the foot of my bed. A little girl, probably around the age of five, just stood looking at me, silent and afraid, until finally she said something about her father being a very bad man.

"Evil," she said.

I never did find out the whole story. I was too spooked. Besides, after that dream, the incidents mysteriously stopped.

Ghost Tours

If you want to find out more about the various places in Edmonton that are haunted, take a tour with Edmonton Ghost Tours, hosted by local actress/storyteller Nadine Bailey. While ghost tours are especially popular around Halloween, Edmonton Ghost Tours will also do private bookings for anything from bachelorette parties to corporate team-building events. They've also done functions for schools, Boy Scouts and Girl Guides.

Bailey has been doing these tours since Halloween 2001. "I love my job," she said. "It's all theatrics, and I love telling a story."

Has she ever had people get scared while touring the buildings in historic Old Strathcona or the University of Alberta, both haunted places? "I've had people who get a little freaked out," she admits, "but mostly it's meant to be fun."

Bailey herself was always a little skeptical when it came to the paranormal. One night, however, her youngest son came up from the recreation room in their basement and said he didn't want to play down there anymore. He seemed upset. And notably pale.

"The man on the pool table keeps looking at me," he told his mother.

When Bailey and her husband went downstairs to check, no one was there. "I've got to say, that creeped me out!" she says. "The first thing I wondered was, 'Did I bring something home with me?'"

How's *that* for an occupational hazard?

POWERFULLY PARANORMAL

Ghostbusters

If you have a sneaking suspicion that your house is haunted, who are you going to call? Ghostbusters, of course! And just like the song from the movie goes, "they ain't afraid of no ghosts."

For the record, the term "ghostbusters" isn't often used in real-life paranormal circles. The new pop culture term "ghosthunters" is equally inaccurate in its description. Thanks in part to movies and TV shows, myths abound regarding ghosts and those who seek them out.

Morgan Knudsen ought to know. This young Edmonton woman works in the realm of paranormal investigations, with a firm called EntitySeeker. Knudsen has seen more than her share of weirdness, but she's quick to bust the myths.

"It's not like on TV. We don't help people cross over," says Knudsen. "We want to take the scare out of the subject matter."

EntitySeeker uses the latest equipment and a team of professionals to investigate paranormal activity. "Sometimes the hardest part of our job," she says, "is convincing someone that their house *isn't* haunted!"

And when a house *is* haunted, Knudsen tries to help the residents get into a better space. By that, she sometimes means an actual physical space, as in moving to another house that isn't haunted. Mostly, though, she is talking about a "head" space. One of the programs EntitySeeker has developed is something called *Teaching the Living.* Through exhaustive research, they have put together profiles of entities and how they interact with people. "Paranormal attacks are a behaviour pattern," she explains. "Ghosts are reacting to you and to your behaviour, trying to claim dominance of their space. We tell clients to do whatever they can to *not* engage with these entities. Don't fight them, because there's a disadvantage. The entities can see you, but you can't see them. One of the best things you can do is just get off the entity's frequency."

That's easier said than done if you're the one living with a ghost. Still, being in a chronic negative emotional state can actually attract negative spirits, says Knudsen, just like it can attract negative *living* people and situations into your daily life. "It's like a radio frequency," she explains. "Being on that frequency can tune you into negative forces that are out there."

In other words, those negative forces exist anyway. It's a matter of whether or not you're willing to feed their bad behaviour by giving them too much attention.

DID YOU KNOW?

Morgan Knudsen's great-great grandfather founded the first paranormal association in Canada. His name was Albert Durrant Watson, and when he published two books on the paranormal, it nearly cost him his practice as a physician in Toronto.

Unsolved Mystery of Epic Proportions

The Edmonton Paranormal Society was founded in 2009 and has conducted over 100 investigations since then. One of its members, Cathy Rogers, has seen and experienced some strange and spine-tingling stuff during her time in the field of paranormal research and rescue. One of the weirdest experiences happened on an acreage just outside of Edmonton in November 2012.

Before Rogers and the other investigators showed up, the owners of the acreage said they had heard a loud "bang, bang, *bang*" on the door. When they went to the door, thinking that the banging signified the arrival of Rogers and her crew, no one was there. And they didn't see any footprints in the snow.

Later, after the owners left and the Edmonton Paranormal Society went to work, all the investigators heard a loud "bang, bang, *bang*" across one of the walls in the living room.

That's when Rogers heard something else: a small inner voice urged her to go into the basement. Against her better judgment, she followed it. Because no one in a case like this should go into the basement alone, a fellow investigator accompanied Rogers.

"When we got down there," she says, "we saw that it was a very open basement, with just two rooms on either side. Suddenly, we saw the light go on, then off. But no one was there."

After that, they went into one of the bedrooms in the basement. Wrong move. "The door flew open, but there was no one in the doorway. Then it closed again."

By the time Rogers and her associate got upstairs, the other team members were distinctly upset. "Where *were* you?" they demanded, explaining that they had been frantically looking for them.

"We were in the basement," Rogers told them.

"You *couldn't* have been!" they said. "We went down there and we couldn't find you anywhere."

Apparently, one of the investigators had walked downstairs and flipped on the light switch in order to find Rogers and her colleague. When the light didn't work, the investigator walked to one of the rooms and opened the door to look inside for them. When he didn't see anything, he simply closed the door.

"But we were there the whole time, in clear sight of the doorway!" Rogers says, still baffled. "To this day, I have no explanation for any of this."

Was that basement a portal into another time dimension, a parallel universe or some other *Twilight Zone*–type phenomenon? Who knows?

Paranormal Party?

On October 27, 2013, the Edmonton Paranormal Society, EntitySeeker and another group called Canadian Paranormal all banded together to create western Canada's first paranormal convention at Century Casino on Edmonton's Fort Road. The Canadian Paranormal Convention saw Cathy Rogers team up with Morgan Knudsen of EntitySeeker to deliver a presentation called *The Legend of Exorcism.*

That might sound like an incredibly spooky topic, but at the Canadian Paranormal Convention, great attention was paid to bringing the paranormal out of the dark and into the light. Also present were everything from crystal healers to an herbologist to a gallery reading by Lynn Van Praagh-Gratton, a popular and positive spiritual medium from New York City who has a gift for communicating with loved ones from the "other side."

SOME THINGS ARE SACRED

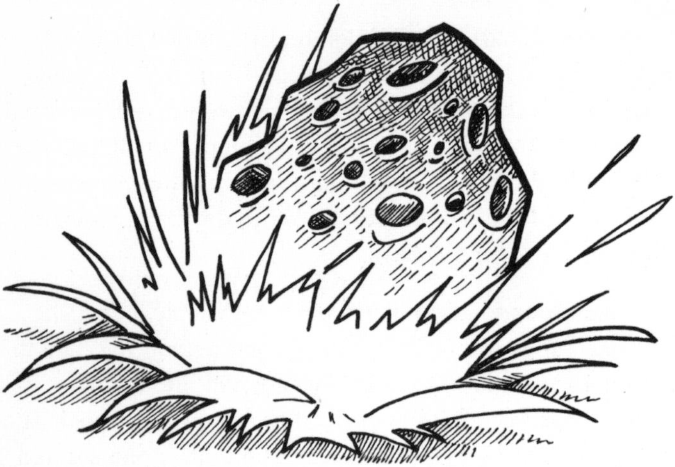

It Came from Outer Space

At the Royal Alberta Museum, in the Syncrude Gallery of Aboriginal Culture, you will find something called the Manitou Stone. The unusual stone is sacred to First Nations people. In fact, the stone is actually a meteor that fell on the border of Alberta and Saskatchewan in the mid-1800s. Where it fell is deemed by First Nations people to be a highly sacred site.

The removal of the meteor is a touchy subject. The Manitou Stone was taken from its landing place and is in Edmonton for the moment, but many—particularly in First Nations circles—say it doesn't belong there, that it should have never been moved.

The Manitou Stone is currently in two places at once. A replica of the meteorite is in the Royal Alberta Museum's natural history gallery, where it is represented simply as a piece of natural history and its story told accordingly. Having the same artifact featured in two different museum rooms is not a common occurrence.

Then again, landing in two places at once seems to have been this meteor's story since its first day on earth.

DID YOU KNOW?

Three or four times a year, First Nations people perform special pipe and smudge ceremonies at the Royal Alberta Museum. These ceremonies are held where the museum has placed the most sacred objects in Aboriginal culture. Aboriginal people believe these items have spirits and are therefore living entities. As such, they require ceremonies as a way of showing respect.

You Gotta Have Faith

Although there is a healthy separation of church and state here, the City of Edmonton officially embraces all religions. City Hall has an "Interfaith Program." At every city council meeting, a prayer from a different faith is read (although some faiths don't actually call it a "prayer").

The City of Edmonton also has a chaplain who tends to the emotional and spiritual needs of any municipal employees who may be in a state of crisis or simply need a helping hand.

MINING THE MIND

Go Back, Way Back

Feeling stressed out? Anxious? You may need to go for regression hypnotherapy. If you believe in the many myths about hypnosis—like how it's scary and can make you do *anything*—talk to Basia Urbanski, a clinical hypnotherapist and owner of Pure Access, and you will get a slightly more factual story. Hypnosis, she says, is simply a way of getting relaxed enough to activate and access the subconscious mind, which is where all memories are stored.

Regression hypnotherapy follows that same logic. According to Urbanski, it helps to take a person back to the first time they may have felt a certain troubling emotion, or at least a significant episode where that emotion was particularly profound. The purpose of regression hypnotherapy is to unlock what might be stored in the labyrinth of the subconscious mind for the sake of healing.

What exists in that labyrinth, exactly? Traumatic memories? Past life experiences? Urbanski admits that she has had experiences where clients are taken back to the womb or into a past life. "When we work with past life regression, if that's what shows up for the client, that's what their subconscious mind offered up and that's why we work with, so the emotions it brings up can be released," she explains.

Brainspotting

Basia Urbanski also does something called "brainspotting." It follows the theory that there are things we literally don't want to see, so we turn our eyes away from them. In a brainspotting session, the client will talk about a difficult emotion or memory while the practitioner moves a stick in front of the client's eyes. The client follows the stick until it hits a point where the client feels an emotion most strongly. That's when the client is asked to keep looking at the stick, keeping the eyes in exactly that position.

If all of this sounds pretty freaky, it is. But it also works.

The inventor of brainspotting, Dr. David Grand, a psychologist from New York City, has worked with victims of 9/11 and Hurricane Katrina and with people from all over the world who may be suffering from post-traumatic stress.

When Urbanski first attended a training session in brainspotting back in 2010, in Bolder, Colorado, she was the only Canadian practitioner there. She is likely the only practitioner in Alberta providing this service.

The Wizard of Odd

As the only city in Canada that embraced the community league system, Edmonton developed a deep-seated tradition of volunteerism that built communities. To get things done in Edmonton, all you need is an idea and a few good friends.

–Shirley Lowe, historian laureate,
City of Edmonton.

PEEKING INTO THE PAST

Do your friends kid you about being an information junkie? If so, this chapter is for you! It's filled with oddities from the past and present. For example, did you know that Edmonton's elite used to live in tents? Or that the body of John Rowand, a Fort Edmonton factor, was shipped in a whiskey barrel to Montréal?

Read on, remember these tidbits of trivia, spout them off accordingly, and you will become known as "The Wizard of Odd"!

How It All Began

Undeniably, the first people in what eventually became the Edmonton area were First Nations. The land also belonged to countless species of animals (and unusual bugs too, like the giant water bug you can read all about in the "Let's Go Wild" section in this book).

In the province of Alberta of today, approximately 45 First Nations groups live in three treaty areas, with 40 First Nations reserves on approximately 812,711 hectares of land. The First Nations languages spoken most commonly today include Blackfoot, Cree, Chipewyan, Dene, Sarcee and Stoney.

The first white person to enter this area, pinpointed at around 1754, is believed to be a man named Anthony Henday (hence the name of the city's latest ring road). At the time, Henday was an explorer working for the Hudson's Bay Company (HBC). It was part of his job to travel across the untamed Canadian prairies and make contact with First Nations people interested in participating in the fur trade.

Back then, the Hudson's Bay Company and their rival, the North West Company, were incredibly competitive. To establish a presence in the area, a fort was established on the north bank of the North Saskatchewan River in 1795 to act as a major trading post for the HBC. The post was named "Fort Edmonton."

Why "Fort Edmonton"? The Hudson's Bay Company's deputy governor, Sir James Winter Lake, originally came from an area in the east of the London Borough of Enfield, England, called Edmonton.

Quite the Feat!

How long does it take to walk from Winnipeg to Edmonton? In 1880, two men—Frank Oliver and Ken McLeod—found the answer to that question the hard way. Over the course of three months, they quite literally walked to Edmonton from a place that was then called Fort Garry (and is now called Winnipeg). The distance between the two is approximately 1300 kilometres. It's a 13-hour drive today.

Why did they choose their own feet as their mode of transportation? It sounds like the punch line of a bad joke, but they walked because they couldn't take the train…because there was no train! It wasn't until 1891 that travellers could take a train from Winnipeg to Edmonton.

Once he was settled in Edmonton, Frank Oliver became co-founder of the city's foremost newspaper at that time: the *Edmonton Bulletin*. The other co-founder was Alex Taylor, the city's first telegraph operator.

Growth Spurts

In early 1891, the population of Edmonton sat somewhere around 300 people, all clustered in a settlement on the east side of 101 Street. That changed dramatically within the year, with the arrival of the first train to Edmonton, courtesy of the Canadian Pacific Railway (CPR). Soon, a competitive movement began for settlement in the area where the train tracks stopped: what is now Old Strathcona, on the south side of Edmonton.

Just one year after the arrival of the CPR, Edmonton was incorporated as a town. At the time, in 1892, the population had more than doubled, with 700 people now settling in the area.

The growth spurt continued into the next decade. In 1904, when Edmonton became a city, more than 8000 people lived in Edmonton. One year later, after the official forming of the province of Alberta, Edmonton became its capital on September 1, 1905.

Then It All Went Boom!

The year 1905 was a boom time for Edmonton. With travel by train firmly established, people were flooding into Edmonton, and the city started to grow super rapidly. Put it this way: in 1891, there were 300 people in Edmonton. By the mid-1920s, only 30 years later, the city boasted a total of 60,000 people.

From 1907 to 1912, the housing boom was so great that it wasn't possible to get building materials to Edmonton fast enough. The housing shortage forced many people to live in tents, not just for a weekend but for a good two to three years!

A particularly big land rush occurred in 1910 because the Hudson's Bay Company was selling off everything north of present-day 118 Avenue. In order to get a city lot, a person had to stand in line and take a number. Land was at such a premium that the maximum number of lots a person could buy was four.

By 1911, most of the homes in Edmonton were being made with stucco. The reason? The housing boom had caused a severe shortage of wood.

More About Tent City

During the housing boom that lasted from 1907 to 1912, so many "tent city" areas were situated on the public lands that the City of Edmonton had to regulate them to keep disease from spreading.

In 1907, one third of Edmonton's population lived in tents. (The city's population at that point was 14,000 people.)

Despite the large number of people living in tents, these tent cities had a sense of order to their setup. Generally, areas were formed according to people's ethnic, religious and regional backgrounds. Think of the saying "birds of a feather flock together."

Even in times when people were relegated to roughing it, aspects of human nature such as ego and classism still reared their ugly heads. And so lawyers and doctors had "upper class" tents. In truth, the exterior of their tents looked pretty much the same as other people's tents, but on the inside they were furnished with Persian rugs and oil paintings. These tents also tapped into the electrical lines and had phones.

Home Sweet Home

One of Edmonton's more unusual homes for its time—shortly after 1912—was the Firkins home. Mr. Ashley Firkins was a dentist who originally hailed from Chicago, where the famous Frank Lloyd Wright was considered to be "the father of arts and crafts style homes." (And you thought his only claim to fame was airplanes!)

It was fitting, then, that Mr. Firkins had the first "arts and crafts style home" built in Edmonton, at 78 Avenue and Saskatchewan Drive. Because he was a trailblazer, his neighbours thought his choice of home was, well, kind of weird. It was a "kit" house, which meant that you literally built the house from a kit you got from Sears or Eaton's.

No matter how odd Mr. Firkins' neighbours thought he was at first, by the 1920s, arts-and-crafts style homes became quite popular in Edmonton. The style was considered more "masculine" than, say, the Victorian-style homes. This "manly" style was characterized by more open spaces, as well as more exposed wood and stone.

The Firkins home still stands today. You can find it at Fort Edmonton Park and, if you believe the details in the earlier chapter, you might feel a tad uncomfortable when you enter it, especially if you're paranoid or psychically inclined. It's alleged to be haunted.

Winter Getaway

These days, it's pretty popular—and easy enough—for an Edmontonian to escape the doldrums and frostbite of the standard western Canadian winter by flying to Hawaii. The first Edmontonian to make the trek to the land of hula dancers and coconuts was a man named John Rowand, way back in the 1830s.

As factor of Fort Edmonton, Mr. Rowand travelled to Hawaii with Lord George Simpson, governor of the Hudson's Bay Company. To get there, the two men followed the Yellowhead Pass to the Athabasca River system, which took them to the west coast, where they boarded a ship that set sail for Hawaii. It wasn't a business trip. They simply felt like going on a vacation.

John Rowand's final "trip" was every bit as auspicious. When he died, he was put in a whisky barrel (after the fat was boiled off his body) and sent to his hometown of Montréal.

Well, that's another way to get away from winter!

Rival Cities

Edmonton and Calgary have had a rivalry going on long before the existence of the Edmonton Oilers and the Calgary Flames, and long before the Edmonton Eskimos and the Calgary Stampeders football teams, for that matter. The whole "Battle of Alberta" began in the 1880s when the Canadian Pacific Railway changed its planned route across western Canada. That route was supposed to be a northern one via Edmonton but a southern path via Calgary was chosen instead.

Edmonton got revenge, however, when it became Alberta's capital city in 1905. At that time, because Edmontonians seemed to vote Liberal for the most part, the federal government of the time (Liberal) decided to name Edmonton as the capital instead of Calgary. Edmonton also got the jump on its rival to the south when it was chosen as the site for the University of Alberta campus in 1908.

DID YOU KNOW?

Edmonton sits on top of some of the most fertile soil in North America. When comparing the yield per acre for Edmonton versus Calgary, the difference is 12 to one (for Edmonton). In other words, you can grow a lot more here in a smaller space.

Take that, Calgary!

TODAY'S NEWS

Largest Loot Stolen

There is no accounting for taste, even among thieves. On September 13, 2013, the online news source Huffington Post reported that Jason Raymond Schell was charged with stealing "the largest loot in Edmonton history." It included hundreds of items, everything from a collector Oilers jersey to a stuffed and mounted mythical jackalope.

Tips from the public led the Edmonton Police Service to Schell's Cumberland-area home in northwest Edmonton, where he was storing a whopping 45 pallets of stolen goods.

To say the least, Schell's tastes in theft were odd. Police found numerous animal heads (including bison, bears and crocodiles!), two bathtubs, a Jacuzzi tub, boomerangs, barbecues, lawnmowers, a stuffed hawk and even an ostrich egg.

He also had up to $35,000 worth of stolen liquor, $11,000 of stolen men's watches and $8850 of motorcycle helmets.

It was suspected that Schell was a middleman for a large criminal ring…a ring with some pretty strange clientele, obviously.

Miracle Baby

In March 2001, a 13-month-old girl was brought back to life at Edmonton's Stollery Children's Hospital after being found frozen outside. While the mother was sleeping, the child had slipped into the backyard, wearing nothing more than a diaper. When the child's mother found her daughter after searching for nearly an hour, the child was clinically dead, with no pulse.

After a team of doctors and nurses spent approximately an hour and a half trying to revive the toddler, her heart started beating again. "I think to be fair I'm using the word 'miracle' now," said Dr. Allan De Caen, a pediatric intensive care specialist at the hospital.

Waste Not, Want Not

You surely know the type: people who buy things, get bored of them and then throw them away. Worse, it's often a whole group of people, functioning as a company. Do the math, and you'll quickly figure out that we human beings have a unique talent for creating garbage.

That said, Edmonton's waste management system has been finding some creative ways to deal with people's propensity for junk making. Take a trip to Edmonton's Waste Management Centre at Clover Bar north of the city, and you'll see a lot going on. It processes all types of recyclables. It recovers landfill gas. It also extracts organic waste for composting. It even processes electronic waste, including DVD players and microwave ovens.

In 2012, Edmonton completed a $4.3-million plant that processes unsorted construction and demolition debris, turning as much as 65,000 tonnes per year of wood, metal ducting and shingles into compost, asphalt and other usable products.

In addition, the city is working on a facility that will turn waste into biofuels. Non-recyclable, non-compostable material will be transformed into ethanol, which will be blended into gasoline. Once this facility is up and running in 2016, Edmonton will proudly be able to say that it is taking 90 percent of its waste and turning it into something useful.

DID YOU KNOW?

Grierson Hill in downtown Edmonton and Rundle Park in the northeast part of the river valley both used to be garbage dumps. Literally. That just goes to show that almost anything can become beautiful over time. Even garbage dumps.

Wear Edmonton

Now you can wear Edmonton! More specifically, you can wear an Edmonton tartan. If you didn't know until now that this city has an official tartan, you'll be fascinated to find out that this tartan actually has a birthday!

The tartan was created by the Edmonton Rehabilitation Society and was approved locally on May 10, 1977, though the Scottish Tartans Authority was unaware of the existence of this tartan until January 2007.

The tartan's main colour (light blue) symbolizes Edmonton's clear blue sky. Green is for agriculture, yellow is for the sun and prairie wheat, white is for snow (and peace, too), and the other colour—gold—represents the marigold. Why the marigold? That is Edmonton's official flower.

Where can you buy your own Edmonton tartan to wear? Head to the Scottish Import store in the city's trendy, upscale 124 Street area. Because the owners are knowledgeable about all things Scottish, they should be able to tell you even more about the meaning behind all the colours in the Edmonton tartan.

Crazy Names for Businesses

Having worked as an advertising copywriter for years, I have come to understand that some businesses have great names and others have names that are either plain dumb or memorably weird. The "plain dumb" category is usually taken up by businesses that believe it's creative to take the first letters of all the business partners' names and mush them together, making names like FraBarRob Industries Inc. (if, say, the partners were Frank, Barbara and Robert).

As for the category of "memorably weird" business names, here are a few of the ones I love in this city:

Doody Hunters: They clean up dog and cat poop.

Nice to Meat You: It's a butcher shop.

Sloppy Hoggs Roed Hus: The folks who run this restaurant are obviously having fun—and with more than just bad spelling. Their menu items are creative, too, including dishes such as Give Me the Hogg Slop and My Ridiculous Fat Ass.

And then there's Tire Shop Plus. That's hardly an interesting name for a business, true, but you've gotta love their slogan: "The best place in town to take a leak."

Neat Random Facts

If you're ever at a dinner party and notice a particularly low ebb in conversation and you really don't know what else to talk about, wow people with your intimate knowledge of Edmonton:

- Edmonton was the first city with a population of under one million to get an LRT (light rail transit) system.
- Edmonton is one of the largest cities in North America, size-wise. It's slightly larger than the country of Cyprus.
- With 275 kilometres of sidewalks and paths, cyclists and walkers in Edmonton have no shortage of places to ride their bikes or take a stroll.
- Edmonton is situated close to the geographic centre of the province. That makes it almost the perfect place to be what it is: the main supply and service centre for Canada's oil sands.

CRAZY WEATHER

Hot and Cold

One of the most unique (and maddening) aspects to Edmonton weather is the grand chasm of difference between hot and cold. The range of temperatures here is vast, to say the least!

The hottest day recorded in Edmonton was 38.3°C on August 5, 1998.

The coldest day ever recorded in Edmonton was January 26, 1972. On that day, the temperature was a whopping –48.3°C. With the wind chill, however, the already blisteringly cold temperature dropped to –61°C.

The coldest Christmas Day in Edmonton was –39.4°C in 1880. The warmest was –8.9°C in 1987.

Perhaps the best (or worst) example of the wild fluctuations between warm and cold would be Edmonton's blizzard of 1989.

It occurred on January 30. At 5:00 AM, it was 3.1°C. By noon, it was down to –25.6°C, falling to –27.5°C that evening. To make matters worse, 29 centimetres of snow came down that day.

Light and Dark

There is also a sizeable gap between light and dark in Edmonton. On the first day of summer, we get an average of 17 hours and three minutes worth of daylight. Generally, on Edmonton's longest day, the sun rises at 5:04 AM and sets at 10:07 PM. During the shortest day of winter, we experience only seven hours and 27 minutes of daylight on average. On that rather dreary day, the sun rises at 8:49 AM and sets at 4:16 PM.

Let It Snow, Let It Snow, Let It Snow!

Edmonton is no stranger to big dumps of snow. In 2011, so much of the white stuff fell that the City of Edmonton went $30 million over its snow-removal budget. In west Edmonton alone, a pile of hauled snow was so massive that it didn't melt away until September that year.

Deadly Roofs

On January 31, 2013, the Weather Network reported that three different roofs in the Edmonton area had collapsed in one week. The first incident took place at an automotive shop in Spruce Grove, the second at the Northgate Lions Seniors Recreation Centre midway through the rehearsal of a group of amateur musicians and the third collapse was at a Brick furniture store in Leduc. Fortunately, no one was injured in each incident, which were all the result of the same culprit: snow. There was a total of 29.8 centimetres of snowfall recorded that month.

The fact that temperatures were on the rise—up from –18°C to as high as –3.5°C—didn't help matters. When winter temperatures are warmer, snow density increases. Put that together with major snowfalls and you obviously have a recipe for disaster.

DID YOU KNOW?

The greatest single calendar day of snowfall in Edmonton was on October 25, 1885, when we were hit with 40.6 centimetres of the white stuff.

Going to Pot?

Have you ever heard the saying, "Everything is going to pot"? What it actually means is that everything seems to be deteriorating or going to ruin. Edmontonians should really coin a new phrase—and it should go like this: "Everything is going to potholes!"

It happens nearly every spring. Ask any Edmontonian about potholes on roads and you're bound to get a real earful.

It's true that the city has a major problem with these road blights. Every year, the City of Edmonton fixes and fills more than 400,000 of the darned nuisances! In 2013, more than $10 million was spent doing just that.

The simple reason why the city is so pothole ridden is because at one point in its history, long before settlement, Edmonton's land mass was a lake bottom. Sitting below the streets are many absorbent soils and clays. Add in our wild temperature fluctuations (from –48°C to 38°C) and you've got a problem. All the freezing and thawing create gaping holes in the asphalt.

Some Edmontonians are fighting back against nature, however, and in a pretty positive way. In 2013, an Edmonton man named Dale Fetterly created a mobile app called Disorder Reporter. It allows people with smartphones to snap photos of problems like potholes and report them. All photos snapped include the geolocation.

What else Edmontonians will do to battle potholes remains to be seen.

We're Not in Kansas Anymore

On Friday, July 31, 1987, one of the worst natural disasters in Canadian history struck Edmonton—a tornado, which peaked at a wind speed of 416 kilometres per hour. In some places, it was up to a kilometre wide, and as it roared along, it cut a 40-kilometre swath through the city. More than 300 people were injured, and 27 people were killed.

To this day, Edmontonians still talk about what they were doing on the day the tornado hit.

As for me, I was driving near Whyte Avenue with a college friend when we both realized we couldn't see the road anymore because of all the torrential rain and hail. When we wisely decided to park at his mother's house just down the street, I called my parents, market gardeners in the Ellerslie area, near Beaumont.

When I asked if they were getting all this rain, my mother said, "Mark, a tornado started to touch down in our back field but then it lifted away, thank God!"

"Probably just a little whirlwind or something, Mom," I said coolly.

Only later, while watching the news—after taking a drive out to neighbouring acreages near my family's place—did I see the devastation of what became known as Black Friday.

Brushes with Celebrities

I got amazing training both with Theatre Sports… back in Edmonton, Alberta (I can't give those people enough credit) and the daytime drama I did. Incredible training, both of them.

–Nathan Fillion, star of *Firefly*

FAMOUS PEOPLE BORN HERE

Take a look at the magazine racks at any supermarket, and it becomes painfully obvious: we're all drawn to the beauty, allure and power of the stars.

As the northernmost major city in North America, Edmonton may seem to be the farthest possible place from Hollywood, with its red carpets, flashing lights and many lurid and always press-worthy scandals. True, we're a long way from bright 'n' sunny California, and sometimes our winter feels way longer than half the year, but all of that aside, Edmonton sees its share of stars, and not just those twinkling up there in the big Alberta sky.

Here are just a few of the city's celebrity sightings and claims to fame.

Our Family Ties

On June 9, 1961, Michael Andrew Fox was born in Edmonton to parents Phyllis, an actress and payroll clerk, and William, a member of the Canadian Army Signal Corps. Because of William's military career, the family moved to various Canadian cities.

Michael Fox first found fame as the young yuppie Alex P. Keaton in the popular 1980s TV show *Family Ties.* He went on to even bigger gigs in the acting world when he starred in the classic *Back to the Future* trilogy, starting in 1985. He also acted in countless other films as well as the popular 1990s TV series *Spin City.*

In 1991, he was diagnosed with Parkinson's disease, but he didn't go public with the news until 1999. In doing so, through the Michael J. Fox Foundation, he became a well-known activist for research into finding a cure for the disease. For all of his fundraising work, he was inducted as an Officer of the Order of Canada in May 2011.

He has a new show on TV, *The Michael J. Fox Show,* a comedy inspired by the life of its namesake.

Kid in the Hall

Bruce McCulloch of the *Kids in the Hall* comedy troupe was also born in Edmonton, on May 12, 1961. Fans know him as the man behind the kooky characters of Cabbage Head or the overly inquisitive kid named Gavin. But students who went to Strathcona Composite High School with him might also remember him as an impressive athlete in track and field and swimming, for which he won two individual provincial titles.

It kind of makes you wonder if he could have made an even bigger splash by showing up at provincial track meets dressed as Cabbage Head!

Millions Love Fillion

Nathan Fillion is famous to a large and rather rabid cult of fans as Captain Malcolm Reynolds in the hit science fiction series *Firefly* (often referred to as a "space western"). Others may know him as Dr. Adam Mayfair in the popular TV series *Desperate Housewives,* with Teri Hatcher, or more recently, as the voice of Johnny Worthington in the animated movie *Monsters University.* He was also Minnesota Ryan in Steven Spielberg's classic World War II drama *Saving Private Ryan,* with Tom Hanks. And who can forget his latest role as Richard Castle on the hit TV cop show *Castle*?

What you might not know about Nathan Fillion—until now—is that he was born in Edmonton on March 27, 1971. He went to school at Holy Trinity Catholic High School, Concordia University College of Alberta and the University of Alberta. At the U of A, he was a member of the Kappa Alpha Society.

Half of Cheech and Chong

Tommy Chong is famous to many as the "Chong" part of the cutting edge comedy duo Cheech and Chong in the hit movie *Up in Smoke* (1978). To others, he is known as a character named Leo on the popular TV series *That '70s Show.*

He was born Thomas B. Kin Chong at the University of Alberta Hospital in Edmonton on May 24, 1938, to parents Lorna Jean, a waitress of Scottish/Irish and French ancestry, and Stanley Chong, who emigrated from China in the 1920s. In his new life in Canada, Stanley Chong worked as a truck driver.

Chong Dynasty

Tommy Chong's daughter Rae Dawn Chong was also born in Edmonton. She certainly comes from interesting genes. Her mother, Maxine Sneed, is of African Canadian and Cherokee descent.

Rae Dawn Chong has acted in Steve Spielberg's adaptation of *The Color Purple* and the early 1980s "caveman" epic *Quest for Fire,* which featured no dialogue...or at least no dialogue that could be understood by your average moviegoer. The language spoken by the Neanderthals in the movie was created by Anthony Burgess, author of *A Clockwork Orange.* Rae Dawn Chong won a Genie Award for Best Performance by an Actress in a Leading Role for her performance in *Quest for Fire.*

She *Doesn't* Love Alberta Beef

Edmonton is the birthplace of perhaps one of the weirdest, most innovative and truly talented Canadian country singers: Kathryn Dawn Lang, otherwise known as k.d. lang.

Although most known for her huge hits such as "Constant Craving" or her classic duet recording of "Crying" (with Roy Orbison), k.d.'s early days were a little more off-beat. In the early 1980s, while attending college in Red Deer, Alberta, she was known for her "cow-punk" sound and look. When she accepted a Juno Award in 1985, her fashion sense was equally odd. She accepted the award wearing a wedding dress.

In 1990, she attracted more attention—and controversy—for launching an anti-meat-eating campaign, which wasn't popular with many folks from the land of good ole Alberta beef.

Law, Order and Identical Twins

If you're a fan of the crime drama *Law & Order*, you'll recognize actress Jill Hennessy as assistant district attorney Claire Kincaid. She was born as Jillian Noel Hennessy on November 25, 1968, in Edmonton to parents John, a meat salesman and sales/marketing executive, and Maxine, a secretary. She also has a younger brother named John Paul (J.P.) and an identical twin sister named Jacqueline. Watch the perversely strange 1988 David Cronenberg film *Dead Ringers* and you will see a scene that features Jill and her sister as, you guessed it, identical twins.

Jill Hennessy's other acting credits include the TV show *Crossing Jordan* as the character Jordan Cavanaugh, Tim Allen's wife in the movie *Wild Hogs* and Jackie Kennedy in the movie *Jackie, Ethel, Joan: The Women of Camelot.* On June 9, 2007, Hennessy received a star on Canada's Walk of Fame.

Field of Dreams

In the world of pop culture, author W.P. Kinsella is most famous for one particular line in a movie starring Kevin Costner: "If you build it, he will come." Recognize it? It's from the 1989 baseball fantasy movie *Field of Dreams.* Originally, it comes from Kinsella's novel *Shoeless Joe,* released in 1982.

Most of Kinsella's books and short stories focus on two things: baseball and issues affecting First Nations people. His first book, *Dance Me Outside,* released in 1977, was a collection of stories about the lives of people on a First Nations reserve in Alberta.

Born on May 25, 1935, to Irish American parents John and Olive in Edmonton, William Patrick Kinsella was raised on a homestead near Darwell, Alberta, until he was 10 years old. He didn't go to school until he entered grade five. Instead, he was homeschooled and took correspondence courses. He didn't go to university until he was in his mid-30s.

While in Edmonton, Kinsella worked at a number of jobs that had little to do with being a writer. He was a clerk for the Government of Alberta. He also managed a credit bureau.

Watch the movie *Field of Dreams* again and you will see that the name of the character portrayed by Kevin Costner is Ray Kinsella. Obviously, that particular character is near and dear to the author's heart. The novel is set in Iowa, not Alberta, however.

CELEB SIGHTINGS

Oprah!

Wildly famous American talk-show host Oprah Winfrey made Edmonton the first stop on her short tour of Canadian cities. On January 21, 2013, Oprah spoke to a sell-out crowd in Rexall Place. The official seating capacity of Rexall Place is slightly less than 17,000 (16,839, to be specific).

While in Edmonton, Oprah stayed at the Fairmont Hotel Macdonald downtown. The staff and management found her to be kind, unpretentious and "very, very pleasant and personable."

David Bowie

Where do rock stars go to watch a concert when they're in Edmonton? Well, if you're David Bowie of *Let's Dance/Ziggy Stardust* fame, you go to the Yardbird Suite in Old Strathcona, and you take in some traditional cool jazz. When Bowie performed in Edmonton during his *Sound and Vision Tour* in March 1990, he spoke about the great tenor saxophone player he had seen the night before at the Yardbird Suite.

I was at the Bowie show. Unfortunately, I don't remember the name of the tenor sax player. Did *anyone*? Sadly, pop always trumps jazz.

Led Zeppelin

What kinds of books do rock legends read? Maybe they go for books signed by such legendary authors as Kurt Vonnegut and John Steinbeck. Those are some of the rarities you'll find at Wee Book Inn on Whyte Avenue, where Led Zeppelin's Robert Plant shopped during one of his visits to Edmonton. There's always a chance that the man who wrote the lyrics to "Stairway to Heaven" was looking for something a little more ancient and mystic. After all, Wee Book Inn also has in its massive collection books dating as far back as the 1600s.

Aerosmith

Where do rock stars go when they shop in Edmonton? Ask Joe Perry, lead guitarist of Aerosmith (the band responsible for such hits as "Dude Looks Like a Lady" and "Walk This Way.") Whenever Joe was in town doing an Aerosmith show—and the last time was in 2010, during their "Cocked, Locked and Ready to Rock" tour—he made a point to visit Vic Lillo at Lillo's Music on Whyte Avenue. Perry is a big fan of vintage guitars, and Lillo's Music has a lot of them. Other music stars that have visited Lillo's include Stevie Wonder and k.d. lang.

Rock Star Dinosaur Lover

Slash, the iconic lead guitarist of Guns 'n' Roses, brought his band to a dinosaur park east of Edmonton called Jurassic Forest. He loved it so much he Tweeted about it. Apparently, Slash is a huge dinosaur fan and really knows his stuff.

Mike Myers

Oh, be-have! In October 2000, Mike Myers of *Austin Powers* and *Wayne's World* notoriety once made a special guest appearance at the opening night of the 10th season of *Die-Nasty,* the Varscona Theatre's famous Live Improvised Soap Opera. The whole scenario happened quite out of the blue. Myers and *Die-Nasty*'s Dana Anderson had known each other for years…and when Mike Myers was in Edmonton, he decided he'd surprise his buddy by showing up unannounced…onstage!

Happy New Year, Seth Rogen!

He's the slacker-type cop in the movie *Superbad*. And the slacker-type stoner in *Pineapple Express*. Long before that, actor/writer Seth Rogen was in one of my personal all-time favourite TV shows, *Freaks and Geeks*, and again he played a slacker.

It makes sense, then, that when waitress Megan Drawbridge served him on New Year's Eve 2012 at a downtown Edmonton bar called On the Rocks, Mr. Rogen was, in her words, "super chill."

She also says, "I treated him like a regular customer instead of like a celebrity, because I figured that's what he would have wanted for his New Year's. Turns out that was true! He wouldn't look me in the eye when I first took orders from his table, but when he spoke I knew who he was. He was drinking Caesars and always paid right away. His wife was also pretty and nice to me."

In the end, Megan couldn't keep herself from being at least a bit of a fan. Later in the night, she asked for a few pictures to be taken, "and he gladly did so, smiling and shaking hands the whole time," she says.

Why did Seth Rogen spend his New Year's Eve in Edmonton? He was actually in Mexico to begin with, says James Der, operations manager of On the Rocks (although he goes by the terrible nickname of "Wang"). Rogen was in Mexico for a friend's wedding, says Wang, and "as a gift, the bride and groom bought everyone who attended their wedding tickets to On the Rocks for New Year's Eve. I heard Seth had no plans so he decided to come for the party."

Hmm. Where would you rather be for New Year's Eve, Mexico or Edmonton?

As it turns out, Edmonton is closer to home for Seth Rogen. He was born in Vancouver.

Brad Pitt

Sex symbol Brad Pitt was in Edmonton back in 2005, while filming the western *The Assassination of Jesse James by the Coward Robert Ford.* Parts of the movie were filmed inside the city's historic Fort Edmonton Park. Angelina Jolie was also here with Pitt during the filming.

Class Acts

Joel Cohen, writer and executive producer of *The Simpsons,* spoke in Edmonton on May 13, 2010, at an event put on by E4C, a nonprofit charitable organization with a big goal: to limit, alleviate and ultimately eradicate poverty in the city. It was founded in 1970 by four of Edmonton's inner city churches.

The topic in 2010 was something a little lighter than some of the other E4C gatherings: television writing.

DID YOU KNOW?

Other well-known Hollywood types have visited our fine city as well. Robert Altman, the director of the original *M*A*S*H* movie, came to Edmonton in 1980 to teach a master class to film and TV producers.

In 2008, a producer of the hit TV series *Arrested Development,* John Amodeo, held a workshop in Edmonton on TV writing.

Cronenberg Crashed Here

Famed Canadian film director David Cronenberg is known mostly for mind-bending horror and sci-fi films such as the 1986 remake of *The Fly,* starring Jeff Goldblum and Geena Davis. Ten years earlier, however, Cronenberg had taken a break from low-budget horror flicks such as *Rabid* and *The Brood* to shoot a stock-car racing picture called *Fast Company.* Starring well-known Canadian actor Nicholas Campbell, *Fast Company* was shot mainly in Edmonton.

Fast Company, however, is one of those generally forgotten films. Good luck trying to find a copy!

DID YOU KNOW?

Chuck Chandler, a former local radio celebrity at 630 CHED, had a cameo appearance as a racetrack announcer in David Cronenberg's *Fast Company.* Chandler was also the host of a local TV show called *Disco Daze* in the mid to late '70s.

More Movie Star Sightings

Many movie stars have stayed in Edmonton and area while filming movies here:

- When starring in the movie *Good Luck Chuck* with comedian Dane Cook, Jessica Alba shot a number of scenes with the penguins at West Edmonton Mall.
- Other movie stars filming in Edmonton include shock value comedian Tom Green, *Saturday Night Live*'s Chris Kattan and another ex-*Saturday Night Live* alumnus, Chevy Chase.
- Conrad Baine (from the popular but often much-ridiculed 1970s sit-com *Different Strokes)* has come to Edmonton many times and stayed at the Fairmont Hotel Macdonald. He wasn't here to film anything, however. He was visiting his identical twin brother who lives in Edmonton: Bonar Baine, who once played Conrad's evil twin in an episode of the much more highly regarded TV comedy known as *SCTV.*
- Speaking of comedy, Leslie Nielsen of *The Naked Gun* fame came to Edmonton in 2003 to receive a Lifetime Achievement Award from the Alberta Media Production Industry Association.
- On May 25, 2013, that same association also brought *SCTV*'s Dave Thomas to the Winspear Centre in Edmonton. He was awarded a Special Achievement Award for the 40th anniversary of *SCTV,* which used to be filmed at ITV's southside studio (now Global TV) on Allard Way. *SCTV* fans will remember Dave Thomas as the Doug part of the McKenzie Brothers (Rick Moranis of *Honey, I Shrunk the Kids* fame played Doug's brother Bob). Thomas was also famous for his hilarious imitations of celebrities such as Liberace, Carl Sagan and Bob Hope.

Groundbreakers

It's about time that Edmonton recognized the fact that we are a great northern city, along the same lines as Helsinki, Oslo, St. Petersburg and Aberdeen.

–Martin Salloum, former president and CEO of Edmonton Chamber of Commerce

BIG 'N' NEAT STUFF

Sometimes big is better. If they were around today, the pharaohs of ancient Egypt would probably tell you about all the people who love to come by and gawk at those super big things called the pyramids. Forget all those wild theories about how they were built by extraterrestrials for some grand purpose. Maybe they were just some ploy to increase tourism!

Some things never change. The race to build the biggest this or that—or at least something that is the first of its kind—is alive and well today. Edmonton is no different. You know that saying, "Go big or go home"? Apparently, in Edmonton we take that to heart. There are quite a few big things in Edmonton. But even better, we seem to like to add something else to the mix…something weird.

So if you're looking for things that are big and weird and the first of their kind, Edmonton definitely delivers.

Except we don't have any pyramids.

Actually, no, scratch that. We do.

Pyramid Power

Edmonton's City Hall is known for its two steel and glass pyramids. They're hard to miss, after all. The taller of the two stands a whopping 43 metres high from ground to peak. Both pyramids serve a distinct purpose. One of them provides natural light to City Hall's main atrium. The other does the same for the chambers of city council. (Neither houses a pharaoh's mummy, alas.)

This powerful re-design of City Hall dates back to 1992 and is the product of Edmonton architect Gene Dub (of Dub Architects). His initial design also included five cone shapes, which were meant to be a tribute to Edmonton's First Nations and their teepees. In that design, City Hall was also circular, as circles are important in First Nations culture, because they allow for space where voices are more readily heard and all are considered equal. That was fine until the press started referring to the design as the "Cone Dome."

In the end, the powers-that-be went with what you see now: a pyramid shape. The pyramid design wasn't chosen out of any reference to mysterious, mystical ancient Egypt. It was simply less expensive than some of the other designs.

That said, Edmonton's City Hall is quite startling in its beauty. Gene Dub claimed that he designed the building in such a way that it would be easy for kids to draw.

Edmonton actually has *two* sets of pyramids: City Hall and the Muttart Conservatory, a botanical garden in the river valley. The latter has four equally stunning glass pyramids filled with some of the world's most fascinating plants. (See the "Plant It" section beginning on page 152).

DID YOU KNOW?

When he was growing up in Edmonton, former city councillor Gene Dub had quite a creative imagination. "I remember walking home from school in the freezing cold and imagining I was Napoleon or some super hero leading a team of people from point A to point B without freezing to death," he says. "I also remember getting down with my nose to the ground, pretending I was one of the ants on an ant hill and imagining how to get around the surrounding pool of water. Architects may not design for ants but being able to imagine other people's needs and lifestyles is an important ability for architects. It makes for more compassionate design."

This Boot Was Made for Gawkin'

Remember Nancy Sinatra's song "These Boots Were Made for Walkin'"? Well, you'd need to have an awfully big foot to walk in this boot!

The world's largest cowboy boot can be found on the west end of Edmonton, at 167 Street and 100 Avenue. Made of fibreglass, the boot stands 12 metres high (four storeys), weighs 40 tonnes and cost its original owner, Dan Semaka, a grand total of $200,000 when it was built in 1989 to promote a store called the Western Boot Factory.

The Western Boot Factory doesn't exist anymore. But the boot still stands proud.

DID YOU KNOW?

During one of her visits to Edmonton, country singer Tanya Tucker made sure she had her picture taken with the cowboy boot.

Attack of the Supersized Pan Flute

Cult pop artist Zamfir made the lulling tones of the Romanian pan flute popular on the soundtracks to the films *Karate Kid* and *Kill Bill Vol. I.* But could he ever make music like the kind made by the supersized pan flute that passed for a piece of public art in downtown Edmonton, on 109 Street and Jasper Avenue?

Actually, that's a trick question.

According to many, ever since its first appearance in 2002, the $750,000 aluminum and steel sculpture—called *Number 23,* after the number of musical notes it supposedly produced on windy days—failed miserably in piping out anything remotely resembling music. Of course, its co-creator, Calgary's Marc Boutin (with his fellow creators Dave Goulden and Tony Leong), argued that people simply weren't listening closely. The problem, said Boutin, was that the constant din of downtown traffic cancelled out the soft and soothing tones of the sculpture.

In the end, it was a moot point. The sculpture was moved from its downtown location in 2012 to make room for a condo development.

Number 23 is currently in storage. It will be installed in a new permanent home sometime in 2014.

Big Bird

Its wingspan is 17 metres. The wing tips are 15 centimetres in diameter, but at their thickest, they are 40 centimetres in diameter. Altogether, this "big bird" weighs five tonnes.

If you're curious to see this creature that sounds by description alone to be something from another world or at least prehistoric times, take a walk through Gallagher Park in Edmonton's river valley, where you'll see the "Peace Dove." This rather stunning sculpture was originally erected in 1984 in a farmer's field near Namao, on the north side of Edmonton. It was a rather auspicious way to welcome Pope John Paul II, who paid a visit to Edmonton that year. The sculpture was moved to Gallagher Park in 1988.

Biggest Baseball Bat

Edmonton is known by many as a hockey town, particularly in the heyday when Wayne ("The Great One") Gretzky and the Edmonton Oilers won the Stanley Cup for five seasons between the years of 1984 and 1990.

It must have seemed like a curious move, then, when in 2001 the City of Edmonton tried to revitalize its 118 Avenue by naming it the "Avenue of Champions" and building an enormous aluminum baseball bat on the corner of 97 Street and 118 Avenue.

No doubt about it. This thing is big. It's 15 metres long. Some have even referred to it as the "world's biggest baseball bat," but Louisville, Kentucky, has a carbon steel baseball bat that stands 36.5 metres tall, in honour of the Louisville Slugger, Babe Ruth. We have to concede that nobody does *big* quite like the United States.

That said, Edmontonians are the proud owners of the biggest baseball bat in Canada.

Big Silver Balls

If you travel Edmonton's busy Whitemud Freeway and keep your eyes open for anything a little unusual, you're bound to pause for a moment and say to yourself, "Whoa! What's with those big silver balls?"

To be more specific, these "big silver balls" are located on Whitemud Freeway on the east side of the Quesnell Bridge. They're actually a public art sculpture known as Talus Dome.

From its first appearance in 2012, Talus Dome was rife with controversy and heated debate. Some have said that it "shines of hope" and that its happy, sparkling appearance brightens their day. In an article that appeared in November 2011 in the *Edmonton Journal,* writer David Staples referred to it as "Edmonton's most expensive, most exposed and best piece of public art."

Others have called it an "eyesore" and complained that this $600,000 "bauble" looks like a bunch of big Christmas ornaments plunked down at the side of the road. Others have gone so far as to call it "a big hunk of silver poop."

Beauty is definitely in the eye of the beholder.

Taller Than Niagara Falls

In 1980, to celebrate Edmonton's 75th anniversary, artist Peter Lewis unveiled one of the city's greatest works of public art: the Great Divide Waterfall. It was 64 metres high, seven metres taller than Niagara Falls. This stunning artificial waterfall turned the city's High Level Bridge into something magical, and not just for that one special summer. For more than three decades, many long weekends in Edmonton were marked by the breathtaking beauty of Lewis' Great Divide Waterfall cascading down to the North Saskatchewan River below.

The project came with a price tag of $425,000, with just $100,000 from the provincial government and the bulk coming from community-minded, art-loving volunteers and donors.

Sadly, the magic ended in 2009. The waterfall had to be shut off because the water it used was chlorinated tap water, which proved to be toxic to fish and was deemed to be against the regulations set by federal fisheries.

In 2013, to mark the 100th anniversary of Edmonton's beloved High Level Bridge, there was talk of getting the waterfall up and running again in some way. One plan entailed pumping raw river water from a raft, but to the tune of a preliminary $2.7 million. Peter Lewis, however, said he was in favour of something a little simpler: a coloured display of programmable LED lights.

One way or another, for more than 30 years, Edmonton could quite rightly claim that it had a waterfall that was seven metres taller than Niagara Falls.

Largest Ecomuseum

What do ancient onion-domed churches, a pumpkin festival and the world's biggest Easter egg have in common? The answer is amazingly simple: Kalyna Country.

Located just east of Edmonton, Kalyna Country Ecomuseum is the biggest ecomuseum in Canada. Established in 1991–92, it encompasses the North Saskatchewan River watershed and extends east of Edmonton toward Lloydminster, covering 20,000 square kilometres (which, incidentally, makes it three times the size of Prince Edward Island).

Within the massive space that Kalyna Country covers, more than 40 designated or informal natural areas provide an endless array of opportunities for sightseeing and experiences you won't find anywhere else. Over 700 events take place in Kalyna Country throughout the year, ranging from rodeos and powwows to festivals dedicated to natural wonders such as sunflowers, pumpkins and the *pysanka* (Ukrainian Easter egg).

Culturally, Kalyna Country is packed with historic heritage sites, including Canada's largest Ukrainian settlement, Alberta's only Irish settlement and some of the province's largest concentrations of French, Cree, Métis and Romanian settlements. It's also laced with ancient Aboriginal trails.

In addition, Kalyna Country includes the famed Elk Island National Park, which is home to North America's biggest concentration of elk, bison and upwards to 250 species of birds.

FANTASTIC FIRSTS

Baby's first steps. Baby's first word. Your first kiss. Your first paycheque (did you remember to frame it?). Oh, and don't forget that history-changing moment when man (or woman) first discovered fire. If you think about it, "firsts" are a big deal.

Edmonton is no stranger to the giddy thrill and excitement of scoring a "first." In fact, over the years, the city has amassed quite an impressive list of them!

Blazing a Trail

- Canada's first female police officer was Constable Annie Jackson. She was made a constable of the Edmonton Police Department on October 1, 1912. Her primary job was to inspire young girls to uphold high morals and manners.
- The first airmail in Canada was delivered on July 9, 1918, by Katherine Stinson, who piloted an airplane from Calgary to Edmonton. And the city's first airplane hangar opened at Blatchford Field in 1919. It later became the first licensed air harbour in the Dominion of Canada in 1927.
- Edmonton was also home to the first planetarium in Canada, when the Queen Elizabeth Planetarium opened its doors on September 22, 1960. Although it is no longer operational, you can still see it today, situated behind the Telus World of Science building in Coronation Park. Back then, the park used to be on the outskirts of town. It was named Coronation Park after Queen Elizabeth paid a visit to Edmonton in 1958.

DID YOU KNOW?

All of the paths in Coronation Park have the same round shape as the queen's crown. It was fitting, then, that the planetarium's design looks like the round ball in the middle of the queen's crown. It's not known whether the design was made to match her crown or merely a coincidence.

First Canadian Broadcast

On May 23, 1927, the first Canadian broadcast was made from CKUA, the country's first public radio broadcaster. The broadcast was made from a small studio at the University of Alberta.

The beginnings of CKUA were humble. It all began with a $700 grant, a handful of engineering students, two windmill towers and some old iron poles. But the vision was big from the get-go: to take the university to the people through the power of the new medium of radio. (This was decades away from television and long before the Internet.)

Since those early days, CKUA kept on growing until the station moved out of its university digs. Along the way, it helped to get a lot of local artists off the ground, including famous Albertan singers like k.d. lang and Jann Arden.

On February 29, 1996, the station scored yet another groundbreaking first, by being the first Canadian radio station to stream online, at www.ckua.com, giving it a global presence and a world full of new fans.

Today, CKUA has one of the largest music libraries in Canada, with 70,000 CDs, 50,000 LPs, and a grand total of 1.6 million songs.

First Aboriginal Police Officer

In 1909, Edmonton's Alex Decoteau became the first Native person to serve as a member of the police.

One of Decoteau's most impressive accomplishments was that he was an outstanding runner. In 1912, he competed in the Stockholm Olympics, where he made it to the finals. A leg cramp kept Decoteau from getting a medal; he finished in eighth place. He had much better luck in 1916, however. Having enlisted in the Canadian Army to serve in World War I, Decoteau was in England when he competed in a five-mile race held on a military sports day. In the crowd was King George V. When Decoteau won the race, King George V gave him a truly prestigious award: his personal pocket watch, made of gold.

In the end, Decoteau's running career ended both tragically and bravely. As a scout in World War I, he was responsible for running ahead of the troop to scout out the enemy. He was killed by a German sniper in 1917 during the second battle of Passchendaele.

As the story goes, the sniper took Decoteau's gold pocket watch. When Decoteau's comrades later killed the sniper, they recovered the watch and sent it home to Decoteau's mother.

DID YOU KNOW?

The first toilet in Edmonton was purchased by the father of famous World War I pilot Wop May. It wasn't as if he got the toilet first because he'd had the tenacity to wait in a lineup for hours or anything like that. No. The truth is that so many people were eager to snap up this auspicious first toilet that a lottery was held. And Alexander May won.

North America's First Mosque

The first mosque in North America was the Al-Rashid, built in Edmonton in 1938. Before that time, the few Muslim families living in Edmonton at that time had to worship in their homes. After 20 Muslim families raised $5000 to purchase the land at 101 Street and 108 Avenue, next to the Royal Alexandra Hospital, the mosque was constructed using additional funds from interfaith organizations that included Christians, Jewish people and Muslims.

The mosque was designed by a Ukrainian architect, which makes a lot of sense when you see the mosque's onion-like domes—they resemble the many Byzantine-era Ukrainian Orthodox churches.

In 1982, a new $3-million Al-Rashid Mosque and Canadian Islamic Centre opened at 130 Avenue and 113 Street. Ten years later, after the Canadian Council of Muslim Women lobbied to have the original Al-Rashid Mosque saved, it was re-opened as a historical site at Fort Edmonton Park, where it is still used for prayer services as a consecrated mosque.

Risqué Before It Was Cool

The first feature movie ever made in Edmonton was called *The Naked Flame,* made by the Corona Production Company in 1963. The film has been described as a "Doukhobor melodrama," but its original trailer takes the hype machine a little further by claiming that it's a film "as bold and shocking as the Canadian Rockies"!

The Rockies are bold, but are they necessarily "shocking"? Hmm…

Actually, the film's original trailer is pretty racy for its times. (There's nudity, or at least pretty strong hints of nudity.) It's also quite cheesy. If you want to check it out, go to YouTube and type in "The Naked Flame Trailer."

DID YOU KNOW?

The first movie theatre in Edmonton was the Dreamland Theatre, located at 96 Street and Jasper Avenue, approximately where the Shaw Conference Centre is now. The admission price was just 10 cents. The first movie screened in the city was *Hearts of the World* by famous director D.W. Griffith, released in 1918. It was billed as "the sweetest love story ever told."

Big Community Spirit

Travel from one community to another in Edmonton and you'll note that many of them are blessed with a park, a community hall and other amenities so beloved by kids, parents and senior citizens. This sort of cohesive community spirit dates back to 1907, when Edmonton became the first city in Canada to adopt community-based organizations.

In 1921 the Edmonton Federation of Community Leagues was officially founded. Today, the federation works in partnership with the municipal government to bring programs, projects and services to folks in the community. The federation might have only one board and one director, but each community league is thoroughly unique.

There are 155 community leagues scattered across the city, each representing different neighbourhoods and the specific needs of the people who live within them.

DID YOU KNOW?

The Crestwood Community League in Edmonton is believed to be Canada's oldest community league. It was started up around 1917.

RECORD BREAKERS

Everybody Conga! Seriously—*Everybody!*

At the 1987 multi-cultural Heritage Festival—the same year that its theme was "Come-Along-and-Conga"—participants set a world record for the longest conga line ever. It consisted of 10,442 people. The achievement was recognized with a framed certificate from the *Guinness Book of World Records*. The certificate currently hangs in the offices of the now-titled Servus Heritage Festival.

Sit Down Already!

On September 6 and 7, 2002, a group of Edmonton comedians won a Guinness World Record for holding the Longest Running Stand-up Comedy Show in history.

The 28-hour show took place at The Comedy Factory and was created and organized by the owner of the club, Bob Angeli.

DID YOU KNOW?

The world's largest parking lot can be found at West Edmonton Mall. The irony is that at the height of that eternally nutty phenomenon known as the Christmas shopping season, it is still hard to find a parking spot!

Obviously, West Edmonton Mall is the favourite spot for Christmas shoppers.

But that's not the only big, weird and record-breaking thing about the place! For more details about Edmonton's most famous shopping mall, read the next section.

Weird West Edmonton Mall

I think Edmonton is so terrific. I have to keep my mouth shut with my Calgary friends.

–the late Barbara Poole,
beloved Edmonton philanthropist

THE LAW OF ATTRACTIONS

The magic happened in 1981.

That's when shoppers and tourists everywhere started talking about an otherwise fairly average Canadian city called Edmonton. On September 15, 1981, Iranian-born Jacob Ghermezian first opened the doors of something he had been dreaming about since he'd moved to Edmonton in 1967: a sprawling facility that was part shopping mall, part hotel, part amusement park.

The realization of his dream was West Edmonton Mall. From that auspicious day of its opening through to its numerous expansions, the mall quickly earned the title of being the world's largest indoor shopping centre. And travellers still keep coming to Edmonton to check out and rave about the city's famous attraction.

The Big One

West Edmonton Mall's mastermind Jacob Ghermezian decided that nothing would be done in half measures. Far from it. If anything, he seemed to follow the saying, "Go big or go home." Hardly interested in going back to Tehran and selling carpets in the family business, he obviously decided to go big.

The mall's overall hugeness—the equivalent of 48 city blocks—landed it a mention in the *Guinness Book of World Records.* For nearly a quarter of a century, West Edmonton Mall retained its place as the world's largest mall. Although size-wise it now sits around the number 12 mark, the mall is still the largest in North America.

Ahoy, Mateys!

Of great appeal to American tourists in particular is West Edmonton Mall's *Santa Maria* ship. This attraction is an exact replica of the ship with which Christopher Columbus sailed the ocean blue (the Atlantic) in 1492 and found the land that would later become the United States of America.

The mall's ship is equally popular with Calgarians. Case in point would be the young Calgary couple Holly and Jake Glast, who tied the knot aboard the *Santa Maria* on October 20, 2012. "There was really no sentimental reason for it," says Holly. "We just thought it was super cool."

Making the day cooler yet, the bride and groom wore custom-made Chuck Taylor All Star sneakers from Converse. The groom's footwear included the date of the wedding on the side. The bride's included the names of the happy couple.

Perhaps the only downside of having their ceremony on the *Santa Maria* was that they could only fit 40 people on the ship, according to regulations, so some of the wedding guests had to watch the action from the mall's second floor.

Fun for Everyone!

West Edmonton Mall is home to the world's largest indoor amusement park, Galaxyland. With a claim like that, you'd expect Galaxyland to offer a lot—and it does. It has everything from a kiddy train to a great big Ferris wheel, from arcade games to bumper cars and cotton candy, candy apples and way more.

You'd also expect it to have some great big monstrosities for rides. And when it comes to that, Galaxyland doesn't disappoint. Galaxyland is where you'll find the world's largest indoor triple loop rollercoaster, aptly called the Mindbender.

Galaxyland also has Canada's first 7D ride. Called the Galaxy Quest 7D Experience, it offers an unforgettable interactive ride experience to appeal to all your senses—or *assault* them, depending on your level of comfort. This 7D experience combines surround sound, 3D effects and the latest in laser technology to produce the heart-in-throat thrills of a rollercoaster with the blood-pumping action of an interactive shooting gallery. There are also robot cowboys and zombies grunting their way through an apocalyptic world. What's not to love about that?

Oh, and if you're the best sharpshooter in the Galaxy Quest 7D Experience, you'll achieve fame (and probably some jealousy) by getting your picture displayed on a big screen for all your competitors to see.

DID YOU KNOW?

West Edmonton Mall has about 30 million visitors a year!

Wet and Wild

It was obviously on Jacob Ghermezian's mind to make a big splash with West Edmonton Mall. How else can you explain the mall's boast of having the largest indoor wave pool in the world?

West Edmonton Mall's famous World Waterpark has the world's tallest indoor permanent bungee tower (only for the brave). It also has more than 17 unique waterslides and play features—and some of them get pretty crazy.

If you're a thrill-seeker, you'll definitely want to try the two side-by-side Skyscreamer Extreme slides. And if you've got a friend who's a fellow thrill-seeker, you're in luck. The Skyscreamer Extreme allows you and a friend to race your way down the ride. And "race" is definitely the appropriate word! These slides are built for speed, with an electronic launch system that carries sliders forward at almost 60 kilometres per hour with two G's of gravity.

Another waterslide in World Waterpark lets you *defy* gravity. The big purple Cyclone slide is the first aqua-loop waterslide in North America to be installed indoors. Here's what you can expect to happen when you're on it: the floor releases, and sliders plummet 17 metres *straight* down before arching into a near vertical aqua-loop. In other words, the Cyclone is only for the adventurous.

Fear of Heights?

If you have a fear of heights and you come upon West Edmonton Mall's Ropes Quest attraction, you should probably just keep on walking by. But if you get a distinct rush from that kind of thing, Ropes Quest is absolutely not to be missed!

Ropes Quest is a three-level rope climbing structure, with the lowest level at 3 metres and the highest rising to 9 metres. Your challenge is to walk through a course of beams and ropes to see if you can make it to the top of this most unique obstacle course. To make it all the more challenging, there are 33 varying elements of difficulty you can encounter. They include walking across a tightrope, balancing on a board and even going through the course blindfolded or backwards.

Is your blood pressure rising just thinking about it all? No worries. The greatest relief about the Ropes Quest attraction is that you're fastened into a harness the entire time. So it's safe. But being safe was never quite so exhilarating!

Little Kids, Big Adventure

If you're a parent, you know exactly how many times in any given summer day that kids grunt, groan and utter the phrase, "I'm *bored*!"

There's a cure for that.

It's called the WEM Adventure Camp. And it really is quite the adventure. In the morning, kids spend time with the staff at the marvellous marine life attraction. They get to learn about the animals that live in the mall's Sea Life Caverns, and they can interact with and feed the exotic creatures.

In the afternoons, kids take in one of the mall's other attractions. That means they might end up skating in the Ice Palace. Or playing glow-in-the-dark bowling in Ed's Rec Centre. Or playing mini-golf. Or sliding down waterslides. Or taking in one of the rides in Galaxyland.

Kids Go Wild

Kids who go wild for animals also love West Edmonton Mall's Sea Lion Encounter Program. Face it: how many other chances will a kid have to get a kiss, a hug and a swim with a sweet-hearted 300-kilogram sea lion?

In the mall's Trainer for the Day Program, kids who love animals get to work alongside marine life staff to learn what it takes to care for the animals. Activities include teaching sea lions how to play Frisbee or throw a ball.

Programs like these allow kids to learn about respect for animals. They also learn the importance of conservation, recycling and taking care of the environment.

DID YOU KNOW?

West Edmonton Mall is an accredited zoo and part of the Canadian Association of Zoos and Aquariums (CAZA).

The mall's marine life staff has worked hard to raise funds for outstanding wildlife initiatives, such as the Vancouver Island Marmot program and the Leopard Frog program.

What's Your Fantasy?

West Edmonton Mall is set up so that tourists visiting the city don't really have to see the city at all if they don't want to. They can just go from the airport to the mall. When they're not spending their days shopping or eating in the mall's many restaurants, tourists can stay in the famed Fantasyland Hotel.

What makes staying in the Fantasyland Hotel different than a night at, say, one of Edmonton's boutique hotels? Fantasy, of course! The rooms aren't just rooms. They're "theme" rooms. You can pick from a number of them, depending on what your fantasy is.

The "African" room has a leopard-print carpet and bamboo furniture. The "Igloo" room includes a queen-size bed in an igloo (of course) and replica ice furniture. The "Polynesian" room has a bed in a catamaran boat. The "Truck" room, true to its moniker, has a bed in the back of a pick-up truck. And in the "Western" room, the bed is in the back of a wooden wagon (and the room has a set of bunk beds in a mock "County Jail" too).

Oh, and there's a basketball hoop in the "Sports" room. And a dance pole in the "Hollywood Nights" room.

DID YOU KNOW?

A Jewish school was temporarily operated out of West Edmonton Mall. Although the school later found a home of its own, for one year (1993), the Edmonton Menorah Academy used one of the conference rooms at the mall's Fantasyland Hotel.

SHOP TILL YOU DROP

Odd Items for Sale

With over 800 retail stores, West Edmonton Mall has no shortage of items for sale. There are tons and tons of fashion stores. There are stores for art lovers, music lovers, book lovers and, yes, there's even a love shop tucked away in one of the mall's nooks and crannies.

If you're on the lookout for something a little left-of-centre, here is a list of just some of the weird, wild and wonderful things you can buy at West Edmonton Mall.

What could be weirder and wilder than a one-metre-tall toilet paper holder shaped like a bear? You can find one at Donna Rose Treasures for just under $175. They also have a Batman cookie jar, a Jesus Tiffany-style three-way lamp and a glass-top coffee table with a wood-carved base shaped like an elephant. The coffee table goes for $549. They also have a grandfather clock for around $4000.

At Artemis, a thoroughly unique international imports store, you can buy a statue of a boat carved from jade for $1499 or a jade eagle for $699. They also have a stunning red crystal ball that goes for a cool $3000.

The one-of-a-kind Swarovski store is a breathtakingly beautiful retail space. The full length of the store was built around a glass skylight in the mall's structure. To see natural sunlight reflecting off the glorious Swarovski crystals inside the store is nothing short of spellbinding. One of the particularly unique items you'll find is a sculpture of brightly coloured hummingbirds handmade out of crystal, to the tune of $1900.

Or maybe you're into knives. If so, the kitchen haven known as Williams-Sonoma has a Shun Fuji knife priced at $549.

Big Money

Perhaps some of the most weird, wonderful and downright goofy items can be found in a gift and specialty store called West Edmonton Coin and Stamp. Everywhere you go in this store, it's stuffed (truly jam-packed) with one oddball product after another:

- *The Walking Dead* card game
- many, many different types of Mr. or Mrs. Potato Heads (including *Star Trek, Wonder Woman,* a *Blue Hawaii*-era Elvis and the classic *Star Wars* "Darth Tater")
- a 50-dollar bill that will cost you $500 (it's from 1937)

- a 20-dollar bill for $700 (from 1917)
- a Royal Canadian Mint coin from the Vancouver 2010 Winter Olympics that goes for a cool $2499. And if you think that's pricey for a single coin, the store recently sold one for $69,000—it contained a kilogram of gold.

Why Not Buy a Meteorite?

Even weirder and wilder items can be found at a tiny shop called Ghossein Rocks and Fossils. This unassuming store sports a simple homemade wooden sign, but look closer, and you'll see some thoroughly amazing and truly weird things, including meteorites, necklaces made of buffalo teeth, a triceratops horn from late Cretaceous Alberta (65 million years old) and El Rathia, a 400-million-year-old trilobite from the Rocky Mountains.

Lost and Found

With a shopping mall that is the equivalent of 48 city blocks in size, you can only imagine that the Lost and Found department at West Edmonton Mall has some weird items in it. Some of the weirdest have included strollers (seriously), wallets, umbrellas and bags of new merchandise (yes, *new*).

Probably *the* weirdest item in the mall's Lost and Found, however, would have to be an acoustic guitar. They also find a lot of metal forks and knives. Only about a quarter of the mall's Lost and Found items ever get claimed.

Weird Whyte

Only in Edmonton could you hop a historic streetcar and ride the rail across the century-old High Level Bridge to North America's oldest and largest Fringe Festival—bar none my absolute favourite summer activity!

–The Honourable Heather Klimchuk,
Minister of Alberta Culture

HISTORY OF CONTROVERSY

There are plenty of places in Edmonton where you can enjoy shopping, dining, nightlife and checking out the sights. But no area is quite as "out there" as the city's infamous Whyte Ave.

On 82 Avenue between 99 Street and 109 Street, this special strip of the city attracts considerable attention. Whyte Avenue is where "it" happens. And by "it," I mean practically everything that's funky and cool: experimental theatre, improv comedy, live indie-scene music, poetry readings, a farmers market and unparalleled opportunities for people watching.

Spend a Saturday afternoon on Whyte Avenue—especially when it's warm but even when it's cold—and you'll spot some of the city's most eye-catching denizens: punkers circa 1977, Goths in black from head to toe, bohemian buskers and even a guy who wears a huge stack of hats on his head, for some unknown reason.

Welcome to the world of "Whyte"!

A Tale of Two Cities

Originally, Edmonton's trendy Old Strathcona area—known for its Whyte Avenue—wasn't even part of the city. It was a city unto itself.

Located on the south side of the North Saskatchewan River, the burgeoning community known as Strathcona was first incorporated as a town back in 1899. Years later, in 1907, its growth was sufficient enough that it achieved city status. It wasn't long after that, in 1912, that the City of Strathcona and Edmonton looked at each other, winked, felt something and decided to get together as one.

Lord Strathcona

An often-asked question—by tourists and Edmontonians alike—is, "Why is Old Strathcona called Old Strathcona?"

The answer is not entirely straightforward.

When it first achieved town status in 1899, the town was named after a prominent man named Lord Strathcona. He was a pioneer fur trader and clerk who had become Hudson's Bay governor, a Member of Parliament and, perhaps most impressively, a railway financier. (At the time, trains were all the rage—every bit as much as smartphone technology is today and then some.)

The odd tidbit about Lord Strathcona is that his name was not in fact "Lord Strathcona." He was born in Scotland in 1820 to the rather bland name of Donald A. Smith. When Queen Victoria elevated this particularly enterprising man to the status of peerage in 1897, he chose the title "Strathcona."

Why "Strathcona"? It was Gaelic for "broad valley," which harkened back to his homeland.

"Our" University?

One reason why Old Strathcona is considered "artsier" than other parts of Edmonton is likely because it has a major university: the University of Alberta.

When it officially opened in 1908, the university was placed in Strathcona. The site isn't where you'll find its main campus today, west of 109 Street and sprawling out for blocks. At first, the university was located in the Queen Alexandra School on 106 Street and 77 Avenue. Queen Alexandra is still operational to this day, as an elementary school.

The University of Alberta isn't considered part of the Old Strathcona district, technically. Taking up five city blocks from 80 Avenue to 85 Avenue, Old Strathcona ends before 109 Street.

Making History

One of the charms of the Old Strathcona area is that the buildings look a little different from the rest of the city—older, slightly more European in character. In fact, a number of the area's buildings are more than 100 years old now, the oldest being the Strathcona Hotel. It was built in 1891 by the Calgary and Edmonton Railway (a rail line that Canadian Pacific Railway later acquired). These days, it's become a popular hangout for university students and hipsters who spend Friday nights partaking in a frothy brew or two—and sometimes getting up the courage to eat a pickled egg. (This is usually the stuff of a "triple dog dare," of course.)

DID YOU KNOW?

In 2007, Old Strathcona was designated as a Provincial Historic Area.

I'll Blow Your House Down!

The Strathcona Hotel was built of wood, like most of the early structures in the area in the late 1800s. It was then decided, in 1902, that buildings should not be made of highly flammable materials anymore. The Town of Strathcona was so serious about this that it passed a bylaw that buildings had to be made of something a little more indestructible.

Taking a cue from the tale of the *Three Little Pigs*, they chose brick.

This Orange Stands Out

The tiny Orange Hall on 103 Street and 84 Avenue was built before Strathcona had official roads, so that's why it doesn't really line up with the present streets or street grids. Go check it out. The hall's location just outside of the TransAlta Arts Barns doesn't quite look right.

It was built purely by volunteer labour in 1903, by members of the Loyal Orange Lodge No. 1654, which was established in 1895 by local Protestants. These Protestants were members of the Orange Order of Canada, a Protestant fraternity with roots in Northern Ireland and Scotland.

In the beginning, the Orange Hall was simply meant to be a place for members to hold Lodge meetings. In 1904, it also served as the point of departure for the biggest parade of the Orange Order ever recorded in Alberta—2500 Orangemen in total.

For the record, the Orange Hall isn't actually orange. It is also one of the few old buildings in Old Strathcona that is made of wood instead of brick.

DID YOU KNOW?

Sir John A. Macdonald, the first prime minister of Canada (1867–73 and 1878–91) was a member of the Orange Order of Canada. So was Tommy Douglas, the first leader of the New Democratic Party and acclaimed "Father of Medicare" in Canada.

STRANGE SHOPS

Hub Cigar

A store with the longest and most fascinating history in the Old Strathcona area is Hub Cigar. It was opened in 1910 by a young entrepreneur from England named Charles Fisher and his two business partners, Eustace H. Cope and Henry F. Sandeman, who were later replaced by a man named Mr. Bell.

Cope went off to Murmansk, Russia, to serve in World War I. While Cope was off battling Bolsheviks, Fisher and Bell moved Hub Cigar and Billiards from its original location—in downtown Edmonton, where the Fairmont Hotel Macdonald now stands—to Whyte Avenue.

A great many years later, in 1999, Hub Cigar was considered the only surviving independent newsstand in Edmonton. At the time, it stocked 9000 magazines and 200 newspapers.

But all of that changed on April 26, 2005, with a freak fire of epic proportions. It was measured at 426.7°C (seriously). The first spark started in the second-storey workroom. From there it blazed through the building's tinder-dry construction and those many, many magazines (which, as one would imagine, were consumed in the blink of an eye).

Firefighters were unable to save this landmark building. However, one item that survived the fiery devastation was an ice cream cooler. Amazingly, when it was unearthed from the debris, it was still in working order.

Return of Hub Cigar

In May 2012, Hub Cigar was resurrected. Located on 103 Street just off Whyte Avenue (on 81 Avenue, technically), this new store contains some really cool merchandise. For starters, true to its namesake, there are cigars. The store even has a cigar club.

Representatives from cigar companies hold talks at the club, whose members consist mostly of men ranging from 30 to 50 years of age. The club has a few women, but cigar smoking still seems to have a macho quality.

What's the weirdest cigar you'll find at Hub Cigar? Besides the classics (i.e., Cubans), they have trendy cigars like the CAO Concert series. These cigars, popular with the Zoomers and Gen-X-ers, are packaged in what looks like a small amplifier (for electric guitars). The packaging alone is cool.

When it comes to magazines, Hub Cigar still carries a lot of them, including some obscure titles you won't find anywhere else. Scan the racks and you'll find magazines focusing on hunting, guns, Canadiana and spirituality (everything from a Jewish magazine called *Moment* to one called *Atlantis Rising,* which appeals to the New Age/sci-fi crowd).

Oh, and there's even a magazine called *Chickens,* put out by Hobby Farms. True to its name, the magazine does indeed focus solely on chickens. And it's popular.

Hub Cigar is also considered an exclusive distributor of soda pop made by The Pop Shoppe.

A Shop for Pop

Anyone who grew up in Edmonton in the 1970s surely remembers Pop Shoppe pop. This Canadian soft drink company started up in London, Ontario, in 1969 and followed a business model that was unique in the world of pop. Customers could buy directly from distributor outlets, bypassing the usual retail mark-up. It was a success. Through the 1970s, The Pop Shoppe expanded into more than 500 distributor outlets in Canada and into the United States. It all fizzled out when the company ceased operations in 1983. In 2004, however, it started to make a soft return to the market, showing up at select locations. Hub Cigar is one of them.

Try their root beer and cream soda. Yum.

What a Shock!

Because Whyte Avenue is frequented by a great deal of artists and fellow bizarre-types, it's probably a no-brainer that just off Whyte there's a "head shop" that specializes in what it calls "cutting edge cannabis culture." The store is called Shell Shock. The merchandise they offer ranges from a vaporizer based on the popular underground comic *Silver Surfer* to a detox drink—Ready Clean from Detoxify, claiming to cleanse your kidney, liver, gall bladder, digestive tract and urinary system—to something called "Zen Rollers."

The latter is used for rolling your own "cigarettes," of course.

DID YOU KNOW?

The staff and management at Shell Shock like to keep their customers on their toes by asking them the "Question of the Day" when they walk in the store. The question is always absurd—for example, "If you could only drink one drink other than water, what would that be?"

Farmers' Market

Where can you go to shop for fresh organic tomatoes, pickled carrots, a big free-range chicken, a "sock monster" (like a sock monkey but a monster, basically) and a scribbler made from a recycled LP cover of Handel's *Messiah*?

The answer is simple: the Old Strathcona Farmers' Market, on the corner of 103 Street and 83 Avenue. Rated as Edmonton's largest year-round indoor market, it attracts a large crowd. On average, the market sees 10,000 people come through on any given Saturday from 8:00 AM to 3:00 PM.

When the market first opened in 1983, it had about a dozen vendors. Today, it cycles through about 200 per year. Back in the 1980s, the shopping action happened in a parking lot across the street from where the market is now.

In 1990, the market moved into its current location, in what is still referred to as the "bus barns" building (because, yes, it was once a barn for city buses). The bus trenches have since been covered up, but the ceiling still has the tracks for the trolley cars.

Although the move to the bus barns was much better than being outside, the site wasn't exactly perfect from the beginning. Because the market shared the space with others (like the Fringe International Theatre Festival, see page 162), the vendors had to remove their goods and their stands at the end of every busy Saturday. Then they had to move everything back in again the next week. This went on week after week.

Another little inconvenience was the single washroom, which was co-ed. And it was shared by all the vendors, all the customers—everyone. Wow. Imagine the lineups!

What's That in Your Shopping Bag?

Here is a sample of a few unique items you can buy on a Saturday at the Old Strathcona Farmers Market:

- Stuffed animals sewed from patterns dating back to the 1920s
- "Quillows" (a combination of a quilt and pillow—the woman who sells them has made as many as 15,000 quillows over the years)
- Old-fashioned barley candy (back in the day, "barley candy" was actually used for toys)
- Einkorn grain flour (it's a rare, ancient grain, 2000 years old, slightly gritty but packed with protein, minerals and vitamin B)

- Unlike other farmers markets, the Old Strathcona Farmers Market offers 80 percent agricultural products and just 20 percent arts and crafts. It also favours local vendors that live less than 200 kilometres outside of Edmonton.

Fire!

On Tuesday, March 11, 2003, a major fire destroyed two of Old Strathcona's historic buildings on Whyte Avenue and 104 Street. The buildings housed iconic Old Strathcona businesses such as Albert's Family Restaurant, Carol's Quality Sweets, New York Bagel Café, and Southside Sound (a used record store much like the one in *High Fidelity,* that 2000 movie starring John Cusack).

Even though the fire was contained to one corner of 104 Street, it created havoc for the Old Strathcona Farmers Market one block away. During the fire, water had flooded into the market. Word spread among the vendors that their usual workspace was under a foot of water. In order for the market to open that following Saturday, the vendors had to come in, clean out the water and disinfect the entire place.

Come Saturday, like always, the market was open for business.

Curio Shoppe Curiosities

Remember that little shop in the movie *Gremlins*? It's that dusty little hole-in-the-wall where actor Hoyt Axton first finds Gizmo the Mogwai. Old Strathcona's Sanctuary Curio Shoppe is kind of like that. You might not be able to a find a Mogwai there, but you'll definitely find some cool and truly one-of-a-kind products.

I quickly spied these items upon entering the dark and sinister abode of Sanctuary:

- Edgar Allan Poe lunch kit
- Skull purses (made by an actual movie special effects artist)

- Zombie garden gnomes
- See-through belly dance pants
- The skeleton "onesy" with a back-flap (cool—and functional!)
- Drinking horns (for mead)
- Toilet mugs (toilet shot glasses, too)

It should be no surprise that the Sanctuary Curio Shoppe has an occult books section. They cover all religions, including Greek, Norse and Pagan and also have darker stuff such as Aleister Crowley's *Diary of a Drug Fiend.* To balance the scales, they also offer a few books on the lighter side of life—Christ, Gnosticism, Sufism, Buddhism and angels, of course.

They also have Ouija boards, cloaks and witchy black lace dresses you throw on when you're doing some sort of arcane ritual in the deep woods somewhere. And they sell crosses—upside down and right-side up—and ankhs, too (the Egyptian ones).

Interestingly, people bring their kids to Sanctuary to look for back-to-school supplies. What kinds of stuff do they buy? Well, one example is pink shoes with a guide for how to make your hair pink (to match the shoes). The average age range of customers is 14 to 45, but the store gets the odd 65-year-old grandmother wanting to appear hip 'n' cool.

The Sanctuary also gets groups of Japanese tourists who don't talk much; they mostly just look and point at the high-heeled leather boots on sale for $600.

But some customers will gladly spend anywhere from $1000 to $3000 in a day.

DID YOU KNOW?

The folks at the Sanctuary Curio Shoppe get some odd requests from people—such as real shrunken heads and real human skulls.

Once customers like that leave the store, the staff smudge the place with sage and sweet grass to clear the negative energy.

Whyte Knight

Although it might not be quite as weird as the Sanctuary Curio Shoppe, Whyte Knight Toys and Games is one of the most unusual stores on Whyte Avenue. Walking up its stairs and entering the main showroom will make you immediately feel like an 11-year-old kid.

Some of the neat items you'll find on any given day at Whyte Knight:

- A framed black velvet Kenny Rogers painting
- A framed black velvet painting of Paul Stanley of KISS, equally cool as Rogers but actually a pretty awful depiction of Stanley, which in a way makes it even cooler
- Vintage comic books (for example, the Superman "Action Comics" era or those old "Classic Illustrated" comics that tackle literary giants like *Moby Dick)*
- Vintage band shirts
- A lot of Dungeons and Dragons stuff
- Magic human body parts (yup, you read it right the first time)
- Two coffins

- And just to throw you a little off-kilter, they also have a distinctly cute Muppets lunch kit. And a vintage Charlie Brown lunch kit, equally cute, of course.

Legend has it they also have bones in the store. Real ones.

Geez...human ones?

Tail Blazers

A lot of restaurants and grocery stores in the hip Old Strathcona area cater to a person's health and wellness. But did you know they have a holistic pet store? Tail Blazers on 75 Avenue and Gateway Boulevard has all sorts of goodies that are truly *good* for Rover and Spot (and those of the feline persuasion, too). The store sells pet food with no colourings or chemical preservatives—even gluten free. And corn and soy free too.

Here's a little-known tip for dog owners: dogs can't digest corn or soy.

ARTS AND NIGHTLIFE

Soap-a-thon

Long before the days of TV shows such as *Whose Line Is It Anyway?*, Edmonton was making a name for itself in the world of improv comedy. Most comedy acts come from the Whyte Avenue area.

And it's been that way for years.

In Old Strathcona's infamous Varscona Theatre (just off Whyte on 83 Avenue and 103 Street), the *Die-Nasty* improvised soap opera has been performing for over two decades now. Special surprise guests have included the famous comedian Mike Myers (of *Shrek* and *Wayne's World)* and Canada's own Joe Flaherty (known for his "Count Floyd" character on *SCTV* and as the dad in the highly touted 1990s TV show *Freaks and Geeks*).

As if to outdo its *Die-Nasty* reputation, the Varscona Theatre also puts on a *Soap-a-thon* that lasts 50 hours! Similar events are held in other parts of the world—such as the 33-hour soap-a-thon in London, England—but none can compare to our soap-a-thon dedicated to a continuous plot throughout.

"We don't plot anything out beforehand," says actress and improv comedian Davina Stewart. "Only the setting is locked down. I honestly don't know who my character is going to be until I show up for the first night of the show."

In case you're wondering, Stewart and many of the other actors involved do indeed stay up for the entire 50 hours. What happens to a person when they stay up that long and do so *onstage*? "You get paranoid," she says. But wait. It gets worse. "You have hallucinations. Your perceptions of everything get thrown off. The theatre seems to get bigger. Once, I couldn't figure out how to get onstage.

"The day after," she says, "it's like you're walking on marshmallows."

We've Got the Blues

If you ever want to do some fascinating people-watching, head to the Saturday afternoon jam session at Blues on Whyte in Whyte Avenue's historic Commercial Hotel. You'll find students, professors, professionals, the chronically unemployed and more, all diggin' the blues. You might even see a woman dancing with a live parrot on her shoulder. (Seriously.)

Blues on Whyte is one of the only nightspots in North America where you can experience live blues music every night of the week. The club has been programming live blues acts since the early 1990s.

The Commercial Hotel has been around for much longer. In July 2012, the hotel celebrated its 100th year with a massive street dance. For one whole day, Whyte Avenue from 103 Street to 104 Street was jam-packed with people dancing to live music and having a great time in the sunshine. As per usual, the crowd was eclectic—everything from families with young children to lawyers and bikers, all dancing in perfect, peaceful co-existence.

All That Jazz

One of Canada's only clubs that specializes in nothing but jazz music has been doing just that for a long, long time now. Since 1957, Edmonton's Yardbird Suite in Old Strathcona has acquired quite the history. Its stage has been graced by an endless array of some of the biggest names in jazz, including legendary jazz singer Nat King Cole (father of Natalie Cole of "Unforgettable" fame), bebop drummer Max Roach and American trumpeter Don Cherry (who shares the same name as the infamous NHL hockey coach but is actually the father of 1990s pop artists Neneh Cherry and Eagle Eye Cherry).

The Yardbird Suite was named after Charlie Parker, arguably the most famous tenor saxophonist of all time. Parker's nickname was "Bird," and Clint Eastwood directed a 1988 docudrama of the same name that portrayed the sax player's talented but troubled life.

When the British invasion came along in the 1960s—The Beatles, The Rolling Stones, The Who and all that *not* jazz—the Yardbird Suite didn't seem so hip anymore. It ended up closing its doors in 1967 for nearly two decades.

Run entirely by passionate volunteers, the Yardbird reopened in 1987, and in 2013, it underwent a swanky new renovation, proving that jazz music is still alive and kicking.

DID YOU KNOW?

The Yardbird Suite was co-founded by a man named Wilfred Watson. A professor emeritus of English at the University of Alberta for many years, he was a poet and playwright who helped to establish the "theatre of the absurd" in Canada. His wife Sheila Watson, meanwhile, was also a professor of English at the U of A, but her main claim to fame is her "modernist" novel *The Double Hook,* published in 1959. According to the Canadian Encyclopedia, *The Double Hook* marked the start of contemporary writing in Canada.

Sorta Like a Rock Star

Feel like being a rock star for the night? If so, do what a lot of people do the day before their wedding day, on their birthday, on a date or when they just want to blow off steam. Go to Rosie's Bar and Grill on 104 Street and 80 Avenue on a Thursday, Friday or Saturday night, get onstage, grab the microphone and wow the crowd. The karaoke experience at Rosie's comes complete with a choice of more than 20,000 songs.

There's bound to be at least *one* that's vaguely in your key, right?

Potty All the Time

On Friday, June 29, 2012, on the northeast corner of Whyte Avenue and Gateway Boulevard, Old Strathcona unveiled its new public washroom. Open 24/7, the facility cost $536,000 and was a great relief to businesses in the area. (Without being graphic about it, just think about how many times you've been shopping and you need to "use the facilities.")

Great effort was taken to ensure that people who had to "go" could do so in comfort. And in safety. The structure's glass walls allow police and passersby see people as they enter and exit the stalls and wash their hands. In addition, the bottoms of the doors on the stalls are slightly higher than other washroom doors, so police can easily see if someone is sleeping inside. On both the men's and women's sides, two exits reduce the risk of someone getting trapped inside by an unwanted stranger.

The city police patrol the washrooms until 3:30 AM. It's also nice to know that city staff cleans the washrooms every four hours.

ECCENTRICS

Walk along Whyte Avenue, particularly on Saturday, and you're bound to see some interesting people, whether it's a guy wearing as many as a dozen colourful hats on his head or someone wearing black leather from head to toe on a ridiculously hot summer day.

Old Strathcona has always been that way.

The Strathcolic

Perhaps one of the most offbeat figures in Old Strathcona's past—back when it was a town called Strathcona—was a journalist named Bob Edwards. Long, long before the existence of the *Edmonton Sun*, way back in 1899, Bob Edwards used to publish a paper called the *Alberta Sun*. Although it didn't last more than a year, it was still around long enough to be given a nickname. Because of Edwards' love of tipping back the bottle, his friends nicknamed the newspaper "The Strathcolic."

Edwards was also partial to drinking something with a little less kick. He and his friends used to enjoy drinking water from a nearby well in Old Strathcona. One day they realized that the water didn't taste so great. When the well was investigated, a dead body was found in the well. After that, Edwards swore off drinking.

Drinking water, that is.

When he lived in Strathcona, Edwards shared an apartment with a fellow bachelor named Bill Halliday. One day, Halliday played quite the stunt. He took some of his roommate's clothes and placed them in front of the window in such a manner that it appeared as though Edwards had hung himself. When Halliday told his roommate that passersby weren't surprised, Edwards left town.

Edwards later surfaced in Calgary, where he published his own newspaper called the *Calgary Eye-Opener.* Many years after that, in 1920, he had an eye-opener of his own. He sobered up, got married and even got elected as a Member of the Legislative Assembly.

DID YOU KNOW?

After the fire that burned Hub Cigar to the ground in 2005, fire crews unearthed the same old well from which Bob Edwards and his friends used to drink.

Robots and Zombies

Take a stroll on Whyte Avenue on the right (or wrong) day and you just may run into oddities as all-out weird as silver, boxy robots playing live music. Go to YouTube, search for "Whyte Ave Robots" and you will see footage of a bunch of robot street musicians playing a tune by the electronic cult band Daft Punk. You'll also see robot dancers too! Few know the identity of these

musicians, and fewer are willing to divulge their names. Who knows? Maybe they really *are* Daft Punk.

Or maybe they're really robots!

As for the zombies you just might find on Whyte Avenue, don't worry; they're just part of the Zombie Walk put on by DEDmonton, one of the city's many festivals and one firmly committed to the cheesiest, goriest horror films ever made.

But think about it: if you were a real zombie, wouldn't that be the greatest place to hide? In a "Zombie Walk"?

Psychedelic Cowboy

According to some of the vendors at the Old Strathcona Farmers Market, a "psychedelic cowboy" used to shop there every Saturday. By all accounts, he was hard to miss. He wore homemade shirts and matching pants, always crafted out of the gaudiest patterns a person could find.

Although he wore something different almost every week, his outfits were always cowboy style—tassels and all—and always utterly, even shockingly, psychedelic. Sort of like a cross between Jimi Hendrix and any "Rhinestone Cowboy" of 1970s-era country music.

No one knows whatever happened to the Psychedelic Cowboy.

Not So Ordinary People

People are growing things in every city in the world, but we're doing it differently in Edmonton. Our economy and our culture, that spirit of openness and curiosity, of urban barn-building, is peculiar. People say it in different ways: this is the best place to build, to create, to get 'er done.

–novelist Todd Babiak,
from Make Something Edmonton website

UNUSUAL HISTORICAL FIGURES

Close your eyes. Imagine for a moment a world where people live average everyday lives and no one—absolutely no one—does or says anything remotely out of the norm ever. It's possible that, for some, I have just described paradise. For most of us with a pulse, however, it's important to ponder: where would we be without the people willing to go out on a limb?

They're the oddballs. The square pegs. The weird ones. They're also the dreamers. The thinkers. The entrepreneurs. The philanthropists. The scientists. The artists. Throughout its history and into current day, Edmonton has proven itself as a city filled with these "types"—people who live life a little differently than most of us. Some dress in Victorian clothes and engage in "tea duels." Or they dress in armour and engage in real duels. With swords. Or they make great inventions that change the world.

No matter how off-centre these not-so-ordinary people may occasionally seem when they're at the height of their inspiration, there is no doubt about it: they are the bright sparks.

And when they glow, we glow a little more, too.

Art the Hermit: Psychic?

Between the 1920s and 1950s, a man simply known as Art the Hermit lived in a cave in the riverbank at Groat Road. He lived alone, with just his chickens for company. For this, people deemed him odd, but many others considered him to have supernatural powers. When the Groat Road Bridge was being built in the summer of 1954, he said something along the lines of, "That's coming down." The bridge didn't collapse as predicted, but it did experience a major failure when that summer's heavy rains washed away the concrete at the base of the bridge.

The truth is that Art the Hermit was probably a shell-shocked war veteran.

Or a psychic?

Who knows!

Wop May: Hero

Wop May is often known as the bush pilot who fought the Red Baron in his last dogfight in World War I (even though some historians say that his friend Roy Brown actually shot down the Red Baron).

Both men hailed from Edmonton.

Another act of heroism attributed to Wop May is the mercy flight from Edmonton to Fort Vermilion on the bitterly cold day of January 2, 1929. Pilots Wop May and Vic Horner lifted off from Edmonton and flew nearly 1000 kilometres north to take diphtheria serum to Fort Vermilion—in an open cockpit biplane to boot!

The story began back in December 1928, when Bert Logan, an employee of the Hudson's Bay Company, was stationed up north in Little Red River, Alberta. After unpacking a new shipment of boxes, he immediately felt ill. His wife, a nursing sister of Grey Nuns, recognized the symptoms as diphtheria, a contagious and potentially fatal disease. The only hope—for Bert Logan and others—was the diphtheria antitoxin, which was not to be found anywhere near Little Red River.

Bert Logan's wife asked two citizens, William Gray and his son Bobby, to travel 80 kilometres west of Little Red River to Fort

Vermilion, where a Dr. Harold Hamman resided. Upon bringing Dr. Hamman back to Little Red River, the doctor confirmed the suspicions. The patient had diphtheria. And it was vital to inoculate everyone else who might be infected. Thus began the frantic race against time.

At Blatchford Field airport, now known as Edmonton's City Centre Airport, May and Horner received the diphtheria antitoxin from Alberta's deputy minister of health, Dr. Malcolm Bow. Making just two stops to refuel along the way, the pilots flew only 150 metres above ground in temperatures of –20°C. The pilots arrived in Fort Vermilion on January 3, 1929.

When Wop May and Vic Horner returned to Edmonton on January 6, 1929, they were greeted by a crowd of 10,000 cheering fans, including a news photographer from New York.

Considering the population of Edmonton was only about 50,000 at the time, the turnout was pretty good.

DID YOU KNOW?

Wop May had only one eye. He lost his other eye in 1924 when he got a piece of steel in it. Therefore, most of his legendary bush flying was done with only one eye. Amazingly, he passed the medical every year. Either the doctor didn't notice, or he pretended not to notice.

Wop May eventually lost his flying licence in 1939, when the doctor examining him realized he had one glass eye.

Imagine landing an aircraft on snow or water with just one eye!

ARTISTS AND WARRIORS

Poet of Churchill Square

Walk through Sir Winston Churchill Square in front of Edmonton's impressive City Hall building, look up a flight of concrete stairs on the west side of the square and you will see a 60-something-year-old man sitting on a bench. His name is Kevan Lyons, and he considers the bench his "office."

Lyons was homeless from 2010 to 2012; now he lives in subsidized housing. Long before then, from the early 1980s to the mid-1990s, he was one of the city's top realtors, but he lost it all—his wife, his family and a million dollars—through a long-time addiction to gambling that began after his 12-year-old daughter died in his arms, of unknown causes.

Now, Kevan Lyons calls himself the "Poet of Churchill Square." He started to write poetry when he was in rehab, he'll tell you. Before that, he couldn't write anything except his signature. Suddenly, writing poetry was what he did to heal himself. When he recites his poetry—at rehabilitation centres, seniors lodges, classrooms, churches and prisons—he swears the poems seem to heal others too.

When he speaks at schools, the kids take to him right away. Through him, the students learn that any life circumstance can make a person homeless, and that homeless people have hearts, souls and real stories to tell.

They also learn that gambling can be a nasty business.

What's particularly inspirational about Lyons' story is his unstoppable sense of passion. It was through this passion that he managed to scrape together enough money to self-publish a book of his poetry called *Poet of Churchill Square* (of course). More than 500 copies were sold in just two months, a story made all the more incredible when you factor in that the book is not for sale at any bookstores. He sells it whenever and wherever he reads his poetry.

He also sells it directly from his "office."

Sir Thomas of Strathcona

Every spring, since the first Medieval Market was held in Old Strathcona in 2001, the Knights of the Northern Realm host a tournament of wills and a market of Renaissance goods. In the market, you can find such rare items as daggers and cloaks, swords, shields, chain mail, armour, jewellery, stones, books, Celtic art, tinctures of herbal remedies and even board games. Watch the tournament of wills and you will likely see the brave and gallant handiwork of a man who calls himself Sir Thomas of Strathcona.

He is, of course, one of the Knights of the Northern Realm. The tournament participants fight using axes, daggers, lances, pole hammers and swords, and they ensure that the weapons are all historically accurate to the 14th century.

You may think it vaguely silly to don armour and talk like Mel Gibson in *Braveheart,* but Sir Thomas of Strathcona believes the tournament can teach any modern person about the good old-fashioned values of loyalty, chivalry and honour.

He probably has a good point. The Knights of the Northern Realm do a considerable amount of volunteer work, such as holding fundraisers for cancer research. It's a staple of their club to serve the community.

"Plus," Sir Thomas admits, "it's just plain fun."

And, yes, it's a serious rush to swing a sword.

Other Sword Swingers

The Knights of the Northern Realm are not alone when it comes to being seriously interested in ancient combat. An Edmontonian named Johanus Haidner claims that he was responsible for starting Canada's first western martial arts school back in 1994. In case you're curious, the school is called the Academy of European Swordsmanship.

Over the years, a collection of outlandish people have joined the academy in an attempt to learn how to use a sword and shield as a martial art and a form of historical self-defence. The Academy of European Swordsmanship runs a tournament every year. In it, they invite those studying other martial arts disciplines to a competition.

The Academy of European Swordsmanship has given a number of workshops to historical groups, schools and even at a bachelor party, says Haidner.

ODD IS IN FASHION

The Official Edmonton Steampunk Group

Many people have hobbies. But some people have obsessions. Visit one of the monthly gatherings of this particular group of people and you'll know instantly which side of the spectrum they're on by the clothing they wear and how they talk. For starters, they dress Victorian-style (think Jane Austen). And you might hear them says words and phrases such as "Darling" or "My goodness." What's more amazing is that they meet at a public place (the Old Spaghetti Factory downtown, in this case).

The Official Edmonton Steampunk Group is part of a growing trend called "steampunk," which is dedicated to the fashions, ideas and innovations from science fiction in the Victorian era. Back then, authors such as H.G. Wells and Jules Verne looked at the technological advancements of the times and dreamed up far-flung futures filled with time machines and journeys to the centre of the earth.

Members of the Edmonton steampunk group believe that we're living in similar times. In the 1840s, there was the telegraph. Now we have the Internet and texting. And that's just the beginning, the group theorizes. And they like to sit around and ask life's big questions, such as, "Where are we going from here?"

Philosophical meanderings aside, one of the biggest reasons why membership in the group clocks in around the 600 mark in Alberta is because its members love the clothes and accessories. They love the idea of wearing old World War I–style goggles, and many of them sew their own duds.

One of the most creative aspects of being a member of the steampunk movement is creating your own steampunk persona. As one of the members of the group said, "You are not bound by being a specific character like Spiderman, for instance. If you're

Spiderman, you're just Spiderman. This is *so* much more inventive."

Yes, and besides, Spiderman didn't exist in the days of H.G. Wells....unless you factor in Wells' time machine, that is.

The group began in October 2010. Its members include everyone from kids in the terrible twos to so-called grownups in their mid-to-late 50s. Together, they get dressed up and attend a bi-monthly Crumb and Tea event at Block 1912 on Whyte Avenue and, in summer, a walkabout at the Fringe Theatre Festival in Old Strathcona. In the dead of winter, they've also done photo shoots at the Devonian Botanical Gardens, posing amid the frost-laden trees (and later giving the photos a tint of sepia, of course).

Tea Duelling

Members of the Official Edmonton Steampunk Group also like to challenge each other to duels.

With tea.

It's something called "tea duelling." The rules are complicated and far too lengthy to include here (really, that's a whole other book!). Suffice it to say, whosoever shall dunk the tea biscuit into the teacup and find their biscuit crumbling first is the loser.

And I can truly say that at a gathering of the Official Edmonton Steampunk Group is where I first heard the phrase, "Earl Grey at dawn!"

The End of Flat Bums

Nora Furber, owner of Monjeloco Jeans in St. Albert, recently went on the CBC-TV show *Dragon's Den* to talk about what she called a "national crisis." The crisis? "Flat bums," she explained.

The solution, she firmly believes, is Monjeloco Jeans. This new clothing store specializes in Colombian and Brazilian jeans that are designed to enhance the female figure by lifting the butt and flattening the tummy. The jeans are inspired by the famous beaches in Brazil and are meant to highlight "the Latin beauty in every woman," she says.

Although a St. Albert resident for three decades, Furber was born and raised in Colombia. And any of the viewers of *Dragon's Den* surely must have noticed that television is the perfect place for her. She has a flare for dramatics.

And for shapely bums.

The Denim King

Remember how popular "stonewashed" jeans were in the 1980s? Before then, in the mid-1970s, another fashion craze was sweeping North America: pre-washed jeans. The pioneer behind it all was an Edmonton businessman named Don Freeland.

In 1972, Freeland, then vice president of merchandizing for GWG (Great Western Garment Co.), went on a trip with his wife Silvia to Venice, where they noticed a store selling used jeans.

When Freeland asked the staff at the store why used jeans were so popular in Europe, he was told that all the young, seemingly trendsetting Europeans wanted to look more North American. Silvia added another fact: "*All* mothers wash jeans before the kids wear them." They were just more comfortable that way. New denim was always so stiff and scratchy.

When Freeland returned to the GWG production plant in Edmonton, the new method for pre-washed jeans was put into place. The new product—something Freeland called "Scrubbies"—was first introduced in a few stores in Toronto. Shortly after, Eaton's store in trendy Montréal ordered 900 pairs. The jeans hit the shelves on a Friday. By Saturday, no Scrubbies were left. Obviously, GWG had a hit on its hands. It wasn't long afterwards that the company was pre-washing 16,000 pairs of jeans a day!

SUCCESS STORIES

No More Dieting?

In 2010, through a University of Alberta spinoff company, Dr. Gary Lopaschuk, professor in the Departments of Pediatrics and Pharmacology, developed a class of drugs that could treat heart disease, diabetes and obesity...and eliminate the need for dieting.

Dr. Lopaschuk discovered that an enzyme called malonyl-CoA decarboxylase (MCD) becomes more active as a person ages... and also when a person is dieting. "When this enzyme is turned on, its activity goes up in the brain and tells you that your whole body is in an energy deficient state, so you should burn less energy and eat more food...which is why when you're dieting your body says it's hungry...but in the meantime, what your body is doing is conserving energy," says Dr. Lopaschuk.

The class of drugs being developed by Dr. Lopaschuk could potentially help people turn their body metabolism back in time to the teenage years when they could burn off their food much faster.

The whole idea came from the butt of a goose. As Dr. Lopaschuk describes it, if you see a goose pecking its bum, what it's doing is accessing a gland that excretes grease. The goose gets the grease in its bill and then preens its feathers with the grease, which waterproofs the goose. This same enzyme is also in humans and is a key controller of energy metabolism. In diseases like diabetes, the enzyme gets activated. Lopaschuk and his research team believe that if this enzyme can be inhibited, it could increase our body's metabolism and combat the battle of the bulge. Of course, they say this in a much more technical, scientific way!

DID YOU KNOW?

Cold-FX, the popular ginseng-based product that darn near everyone seems to take at the first sign of catching a cold, was originally manufactured by Afexa Life Sciences Inc. (once called CV Technologies Inc.). Their headquarters? Edmonton.

In 2011, the company was acquired by Valeant Pharmaceuticals International, which has its headquarters in Laval, Québec.

The Nutty Professor

In his classic screwball comedy *The Nutty Professor* (1963), Jerry Lewis played a chemistry professor fiddling with science of Jekyll and Hyde proportions. A chemistry professor at the University of Alberta has also had some "nutty" teaching methods in the classroom—nutty but highly effective!

Dr. Glen Loppnow is highly regarded in the world of scientific research for his work in the field of measuring damage in nucleic acids such as DNA and RNA. Such damage, he has theorized, can cause certain types of diseases. In the classroom, he's equally innovative. He has his students produce music videos about entropy in the universe or has them create rap songs about climate change.

A Cure for Diabetes?

Edmontonians are definitely inventive!

A research team from the University of Alberta recently discovered a procedure that has made a huge and positive change in the lives of hundreds of Edmontonians living with diabetes.

These groundbreaking researchers transplanted islet cells from human pancreases into patients with Type I diabetes. Many of the patients who have received this treatment are able to lead improved lives and no longer have to depend on daily injections of insulin.

The procedure is known as The Edmonton Protocol, and it has gained national recognition. Of course, this isn't the first time Edmonton scientists have achieved something big in the battle against diabetes. In 1923, Edmonton biochemist Dr. James Collip shared the 1923 Nobel Prize with fellow researchers Frederick Banting and Charles Best for discovering insulin.

Slumlord Millionaire?

Edmonton's Sheetal Mehta got her BA in political science from the University of Alberta in 1994. After a while, she was head of Venture Capital for Microsoft, CEO of Innovative Social Ventures. A little later in her career, she changed direction somewhat and became co-founder of Shivia Microfinance, a UK charity that helps people in the villages and slums of India set up businesses.

The Polar Express

As if life in Edmonton isn't cold enough during its five to six months of winter, Dr. Gregory Thiemann from the University of Alberta's Faculty of Biological Sciences has committed endless hours in sub-zero temperatures to researching the lives of polar bears in the Arctic. His work has helped to create a deeper understanding of the changing Arctic climate and the impacts of humans on the north.

Plus, he gets to work with polar bears. Seriously, how cool is that? (Well, *cold,* really.)

Quirky Science

University of Alberta Faculty of Science alumnus Jay Ingram was the host of CBC Radio's popular science program *Quirks and Quarks* for 13 years. You may also recognize him as the co-host and producer of Discovery Channel's *Daily Planet.* He has also written eight books, three of which have won Canadian Science Writers' Awards.

Ingram's brain-busting books tell tales such as the one about the epileptic who underwent brain surgery and came out of it with no ability to store new memories. The books also seek to answer questions to why, for example, amputees often feel the pangs of a phantom limb.

The author returned to the University of Alberta in his home city in October 2013 to discuss something even more unusual: prions. A prion is a brain molecule that changes its shape and begins to infect the cells around it. At present, no one knows exactly why this happens, although as Ingram explained in his talk, researchers are scrambling to find the answers.

Not-so-fabulous Furball?

When Krista Castellarin appeared on CBC-TV's *Dragon's Den* to do a pitch for her franchise pet grooming company Fabulous Furballs, she impressed investor Bruce Croxon enough to receive an offer of $200,000 for 10 percent of her company.

Sadly, the offer was later withdrawn. There were rumours that her income figure of $1.3 million was inflated. But that wasn't the official statement given by *Dragon's Den.* Spokesperson Jane Collins simply said, "The way it is here is it's sort of a-deal-is-a-deal, and from that point on, it's really between the entrepreneurs themselves and the dragons."

The withdrawn offer had some not-so-fabulous ripple effects. Mike and Liz Dussault, the owners of a Sherwood Park shop that had recently become part of Fabulous Furballs, distanced themselves from the franchise. The couple is still running a pet grooming salon but are doing so independently.

Sometimes fame can really bite.

THE GOOD, THE BAD AND THE PECULIAR

The Voice for Justice

During the 1970s and 1980s, many people living in and around Edmonton remember the voice of Eddie Keen. As a radio commentator on the famed 630 CHED, Eddie Keen stood up for the little people. Thanks to his efforts, motorists were saved from a major scandal involving seemingly trustworthy Edmonton auto dealers tampering with odometers. The fact that he was also a columnist for the *Edmonton Sun* gave Keen even more power in outing the corrupt.

Sometimes his belief in the dignity of the little guy was challenging to public opinion, at least until people caught on. Such was the case when he led the campaign to appeal the life sentence of a young man from Stony Plain (just west of Edmonton) named Ross Davis who was in jail for stabbing to death his stepfather, Frank Koble, on April 1, 1976. It turned out that Davis, then 16 years old, was simply standing up for his little sister, age 13, after Koble had sexually assaulted her. Keen led the campaign for a good five years, until the solicitor general at the time, Robert Kaplan, granted Davis a pardon.

Super Serious Coffee Drinker

In summer of 2013, Monica Kavanagh bought 800 cups of coffee at Tim Hortons at 98 Street and 153 Avenue. She wasn't cramming for an exam and needed to pull an all-nighter. Nor was she incredibly thirsty.

This particular purchase was a random act of human kindness. Kavanagh simply did it so the first 800 people to arrive after her could have a free coffee.

King of the Strip

Just off Jasper Avenue on 105 Street—across the street from a Presbyterian church—is a mural on the side of the building that houses a business called Chez Pierre, which holds the dubious honour for being the city's first nude dance bar. The somewhat lecherous-looking figure in the mural is Pierre.

He's a real man, not just a character. In two years, Pierre Cochard will be celebrating his 90th birthday. He first opened his infamous establishment over 40 years ago. In 2010, Cochard announced that he was getting too old for any kind of hands-on management of his club. So he handed that duty over to his 21-year-old grandson Jesse, a part-time student of management studies at Grant MacEwan University.

The Princess Bride

And now here's a story about a *not*-so-kind Edmonton woman who once stayed at the Fairmont Hotel Macdonald. Although the always incredibly professional staff at the hotel is usually able to handle and accommodate all kinds of variables, they actually had to say "no" to one person—a woman they call the "Princess Bride."

To say the least, when the Princess Bride was celebrating her wedding in the hotel in 2010, her request was a tad unreasonable. She wanted them to paint the ceilings. Oh, and she also wanted to bring her own chandeliers!

This begs the obvious question: who brings their own chandeliers when they travel? What average person even has chandeliers to bring in the first place?

Unique Twitter Handles

In Edmonton, like so many other cities around the world, the interest in social media keeps growing and growing. Although there are fascinating Twitter handles anywhere in the world, Edmonton (hashtag: #yeg) has some particularly bizarre ones.

Someone goes by the handle of @yegmagpie. In this person's tweets, he or she pretends to be a bird. A magpie, of course. And the number of Twitter followers is nearly 1500 and counting. There's also one called @yegcoyote, who, that's right, pretends to be a coyote, and a @YegSquirrel too. It sort of makes you wonder which one came first…

City of Champions

The biggest difference between L.A. and Edmonton was that instead of people looking at me I was looking at them.

–Wayne Gretzky

GO FOR THE GOLD

Edmontonians are good sports. It doesn't matter that the Edmonton Oilers have yet to reclaim their former glory of winning their five Stanley Cup championships between 1984 and 1990 or that the Edmonton Eskimos aren't the same football team that won a record five Grey Cups in a row between 1978 and 1982. Fans still come out to the games. But what about the other sports in Edmonton?

What about basketball or baseball? Or boxing? Or wrestling? Or roller derby? Or a game of cards, for that matter?

Dig deeper and you'll find out that Edmonton has some interesting happenings in the wonderful world of sports.

Is Vandalism a Sport?

In the fall of 2013, pranksters defamed various "City of Champions" signs around Edmonton. In place of the phrase "City of Champions" were others such as "City of Speed Traps," "Road Construction City" and another that simply said, "Suck it, Calgary."

It Was in the Cards

Edmontonian Peter Jones is the only Canadian in history to win an Olympic gold medal.

For Bridge.

Yes, you read that correctly. Bridge—the card game—is actually an Olympic spectator sport (although it's hard to imagine stands full of screaming fans cheering on the action). Peter Jones won his prestigious gold medal during the 2002 Winter Olympic Games in Salt Lake City.

Edmonton's Best Team Ever?

Everyone and their dog seems to know about the Edmonton Oilers and the Edmonton Eskimos. Sadly, not many people know about a team called the Edmonton Grads. That is odd considering that the Edmonton Grads continue to hold the North American record for the sports team with the best winning percentage of all time.

The Edmonton Grads were a women's basketball team with humble beginnings and a great big story to tell. It all began when the senior girls basketball team of McDougall Commercial High School in Edmonton won the Alberta High School Provincial championship in the school year of 1914–15. After graduating, the team asked their school coach J. Percy Page if he would continue to coach them. After all, they were definitely willing to keep competing. It was fitting that this group of recent high school graduates became known as the Edmonton Grads. The team name they had before that was the Commercial Graduates Basketball Club. Not quite as catchy!

The newly titled team scored a record of over 500 wins and only 20 losses between the years of 1915 and 1940. They won their first Canadian title in 1922. The following year they won their first international competition, the Underwood Trophy ("Underwood" as in the typewriter). The Edmonton Grads lost the Underwood Trophy only once by the time of the team's official demise in 1940.

The Edmonton Grads also have the distinction of winning every match they had in the Olympic Games from 1924 to 1936—27 Olympic matches in total.

DID YOU KNOW?

The Edmonton Grads' successes were declared a National Historic Event in 1976. Two years later, Parks Canada dedicated a plaque in their honour, which is located at the southeast entrance of Commonwealth Stadium. In 1980, the Canadian Basketball Hall of Fame inducted the team's entire roster of players.

More Girl Power

Edmonton sports history also boasts a talented women's hockey team. They were called the Jasper Place Rustlers because they represented the Town of Jasper Place, which used to be a town unto itself until it was amalgamated with Edmonton in 1964.

The Rustlers were the Dominion of Canada champions for two years in a row, in 1933 and '34. Their coach was Corwin Ray (C.R.) Tufford. Tufford Way in Terwillegar Park was named in honour of his many contributions, which included serving as a councillor for Jasper Place.

The Royal Washroom

The 11th Commonwealth Games were held August 3 to 12, 1978, at Commonwealth Stadium, which was built specifically for the occasion. Knowing that the Queen of England would be making an appearance at the games, the stadium even had a "royal washroom" set up. Legend has it she never used it. Surely the regular washrooms got a workout! Approximately 1500 athletes from 46 countries came to Edmonton to compete in the games.

Canada came out on top. That was the year the country was ranked number one in medals, picking up 109 in total: 45 gold, 31 silver and 33 bronze. It was the first and only time such a feat had happened since the Commonwealth Games first began in 1930.

Triumph and Tragedy

Just a few years after the Commonwealth Games, Edmonton hosted another large scale sporting event: the 1983 Summer Universiade. Taking place from July 1 to 12, with more than 2400 athletes from 73 countries participating, it once again put Edmonton on the map.

The Universiade was also known far and wide for a tragedy.

While attempting a reverse 3½ in the tuck position during the competition, Soviet diver Sergei Chalibashvili hit his head on the platform. The accident left him in a coma for eight days. He never regained consciousness and died of heart failure.

World's Longest Hockey Game

On January 24, 2013, Brent Saik was officially recognized by royalty when he was awarded a Diamond Jubilee Medal for organizing the world's longest hockey game, not once but four times—and doing it all for cancer research.

The first time it happened was in 2003, when Saik and 39 other hockey players set the new Guinness World Record by playing 82 hours of hockey on the regulation-size rink in the backyard of his acreage in Strathcona County. The second time, Saik and his fellow players more than outdid themselves when they played for 240 hours in 2005, 241 hours and 21 minutes in 2008, and 242 hours in February 2011.

Saik is team optometrist for the Edmonton Oilers and Edmonton Eskimos and president of the Alberta Sports Vision Institute. His unique philanthropic work was initially inspired by his father Terry, who lost his battle to cancer in 1991. Saik's efforts were further spurred on by the loss of his wife Susan to cancer in 2003.

Over the years, Saik's games have raised $2 million for the Cross Cancer Institute in Edmonton.

SPORTS LEGENDS

The Great One

He has been called "the greatest hockey player ever." Although he was born and raised in Brantford, Ontario, Wayne Douglas Gretzky (born January 26, 1961) spent what were arguably his most famous years in Edmonton.

Gretzky played 20 seasons in the National Hockey League (NHL), from 1979 to 1999. From 1979 to 1988, he was the star player of the Edmonton Oilers. He was also the team captain from 1983 to 1988. Undeniably, he had quite a few star players at his side, including Glenn Anderson, Jari Kurri, Paul Coffey, goaltender Grant Fuhr and Edmonton's own Mark Messier. All of these players went on to become Hockey Hall of Famers.

The Edmonton Oilers achieved Hockey Hall of Fame status, too. The team was noted as a "dynasty" for winning the Stanley Cup playoffs on five occasions in just seven years, from 1983 to 1988 and in 1990.

By 1990, Edmonton's favourite hockey player was no longer a part of the city. In 1988, just two hours after the Oilers won the Stanley Cup, Wayne's father Walter told his son that he'd been traded to the Los Angeles Kings. The news wasn't a surprise to some, since The Great One had recently married actress Janet Jones, who lived in none other than Los Angeles.

Edmonton never forgot Wayne Gretzky, however. In October 1999, one of the city's busiest freeways, Capilano Drive—just east of the Oilers' ice rink in Rexall Place—was renamed "Wayne Gretzky Drive." There is also a rush-hour bus route numbered "99," which runs on Wayne Gretzky Drive.

Gretzky is considered the leading point-scorer in NHL history. In addition, he is the only NHL player to total over 200 points in one season, a feat he accomplished not just once but four times! He is also a five-time winner of the Lady Byng Trophy, awarded for sportsmanship and performance. Listing Gretzky's many other awards and accomplishments would simply take too long, and we're trying to be kind to trees.

He retired from hockey in 1999.

Cold Classic

Never let it be said that Edmontonians aren't serious hockey fans. Why else would 57,167 fans have flocked to Commonwealth Stadium on November 23, 2003, and braved it out during temperatures of –18°C, and with the wind chill factor, –30°C?

The return of The Great One was part of the draw—the one-night-only comeback of Wayne Gretzky. He'd made the trip to his old stomping grounds to play in the Heritage Classic—the first NHL game played outdoors as part of the regular season play. Before an official game was played by the league's then-current teams of the Edmonton Oilers and the Montreal Canadiens, there was a MegaStars game featuring the best former players from both teams. Guy Lafleur led the Canadiens, and Gretzky led the Oilers. The final score of that MegaStars game was Oilers 2, Canadiens 0.

Peter Puck

Perhaps one of the most loved and hated men in Edmonton's sports history would have to be Peter Pocklington, known to many as "Peter Puck." The nickname comes from Pocklington's long-time association with hockey and, more specifically, with the Edmonton Oilers.

Pocklington bought part ownership of the Oilers in 1976, back when they were in the World Hockey Association (WHA). Within a year, Pocklington bought out his partner, Nelson Skalbania, who became a major player in Pocklington's life for one key reason: in 1978, Skalbania offered Pocklington the rights to a young hockey player named Wayne Gretzky, then 17 years old. One year later, the Oilers entered the NHL. Just a few years after that, Gretzky and the Oilers were making hockey history.

Peter Puck went on to gain considerable fame, too. In many ways, he was Edmonton's answer to Donald Trump. Over the course of two whirlwind decades of wheeling and dealing, Pocklington owned much of the local sporting world. In baseball he owned the Edmonton Trappers. In soccer he had the Edmonton Drillers. He also owned the Kamloops Junior Oilers, in the Western Hockey League.

Pocklington also diversified into a vehicle dealership in downtown Toronto (Elgin Ford), one of Canada's largest trust companies (Fidelity Trust), an Edmonton-based meat packing company (Gainers) and one of the largest retailers of dairy products in western Canada (Palm Dairies). In addition, he had massive real estate holdings throughout Alberta and Ontario.

His business empire was so great that at one time it exceeded $2 billion in sales.

Of course, Peter Puck is also reviled in many circles as the man who traded Wayne Gretzky to the Los Angeles Kings, right when hockey fever was at its height in Edmonton.

In October 1998, Pocklington and his wife Eva moved to California. Ten years later, a number of Pocklington's business ventures landed him in a series of lawsuits. One of them resulted in not one but three raids on his home, during which a number of his wife's possessions were seized but were eventually returned. Peter Puck then decided that the best way to protect against mounting legal fees was to declare personal bankruptcy.

In 2013, a California judge sentenced Pocklington to six months in prison and an additional six months of house arrest for breaching his probation on a previous conviction related to bankruptcy fraud.

DID YOU KNOW?

Peter Pocklington once spent 11 hours face to face with a gunman who broke into Pocklington's home in April 1982 and took hostages for a ransom negotiated at $2 million. The gunman was Mirko Petrovic, a Yugoslav immigrant. The ransom was never paid because police managed to sneak into Pocklington's home and shoot Petrovic, wounding him.

They also accidentally shot Pocklington in the process, but he received only minor injuries. Petrovic recovered from his wounds, too, but he ended up serving five years in an Alberta prison. Upon his release he was returned to Yugoslavia.

Billionaire Hockey Fan

Daryl Katz may have graduated from the University of Alberta with a law degree in 1985, but he was as good as broke at the time. But he had an idea. The son of a pharmacist, he visited the head office of a big name in pharmaceuticals, McKesson, to pitch buying up under-performing drugstore chains. Under Katz's management, the company turned around and then some.

The Rexall drugstore chain turned Daryl Katz into a billionaire. According to *Forbes* magazine, he was worth $2.6 billion as of March 2013.

One of Katz's pet purchases was a hockey team, the Edmonton Oilers, which only made sense considering his boyhood love of hockey. Not satisfied with the Oilers' current home (Rexall Place, formerly the Northlands Coliseum), he met with architects and lobbied city officials to build the Katz Centre, a hockey arena that city council finally approved in January 2013, after years of debate.

As for the home that Katz lives in, to simply call it a "riverfront mansion" would be an understatement. Located at 4 Valleyview Point in the city's Parkview neighbourhood, this $20-million mansion is one of the largest homes in Edmonton, boasting almost 2400 square metres. The great room is made of 90-kilogram blocks of ancient Italian limestone. The property also includes two swimming pools.

DID YOU KNOW?

Daryl Katz bought the multi-million-dollar home next to his and demolished it to build what he says is a practice ice rink for his two kids.

A Tiger of a Man

If you think that "Tiger Goldstick" is an unlikely name for a sports celebrity, you have to consider that the name he was born with on August 5, 1915, was even less likely for marquee status. Cecil Goldstick was the son of mother Bessie and father Hyman, who was Edmonton's first rabbi. After earning the nickname of "Tiger" for his feisty personality, Cecil went on to become an icon to a generation of Edmonton sports fans and kids, as a sports announcer for CFRN Radio and TV and as host of *Tiger's Den* on the popular local after-school children's show, *Popcorn Playhouse.*

To many, he was known as the colourful-and-sometimes-crusty character who talked to kids about traffic safety from his "tiger's den," but the truth is that despite being only 1.6 metres (5 feet, 4 inches) tall, Tiger Goldstick once showed promise as a wrestler. In fact, he showed so much promise that he earned a place on the city's boxing and wrestling commission's honours roll.

It was through wrestling that Cecil earned his nickname. "I used to wrestle in the navy," Goldstick once explained to a writer from the *Edmonton Journal*. It was felt that he needed a proper name, he explained, so one day before a match he was introduced as "the Tiger of Western Canada."

It proved to be a fitting nickname. For years, Tiger Goldstick was known for getting into fights with officials at sporting events. If he didn't like a call, he'd say so.

Tiger had a heart of gold, however, especially when it came to kids. Because he grew up during the Depression and knew what it was like to have a love for sports but no stick or bat, he began collecting sports equipment to distribute to kids. In 1990, he was inducted into the Order of Canada for his work in helping kids.

Tiger Goldstick passed away on February 3, 2006, at the age of 90.

DID YOU KNOW?

The movie *Running Brave*, starring heartthrob Robby Benson, was filmed in Edmonton in 1982, at Commonwealth Stadium. Listen and watch for scenes that include another of the city's most beloved celebrity sportscasters, 630 CHED's Bryan Hall. His role isn't much of a stretch. He plays—what else—a sportscaster!

HAVE A BALL

Major League Fall

Todd Ruben Cruz was an American Major League Baseball player who spent six seasons in the majors from 1978 to 1984, with teams such as the Philadelphia Phillies, Kansas City Royals, California Angels, Chicago White Sox and Baltimore Orioles.

So why is he in this book, you ask? Well, when Cruz suffered a back injury that sidelined him for an entire season in 1981, he ended up playing with the minor league Triple A team the Edmonton Trappers! (The Trappers no longer exist; since they folded, we've had the Cracker Cats, the Capitals and now the Edmonton Prospects, a collegiate summer team.)

Cruz's time here wasn't so great. After playing his first game in Edmonton on May 18, 1981, Cruz was apparently so depressed and homesick for his wife—or so the story goes—that in the wee hours of the following day he got drunk, broke into the Hudson's Bay building downtown and stole a bunch of watches. When Cruz showed up for his next game, someone in the stands yelled out to him, "What time is it?"

The whole episode landed Cruz in court. Charged with breaking and entering and theft over $200, he took a plea bargain; he pleaded to *attempted* breaking and entering and theft. The judge gave him a conditional discharge with nine months probation, which meant he wouldn't end up with a criminal record.

Cruz played only eight games with the Edmonton Trappers that season. Two years later he was playing with the Baltimore Orioles when they won the World Series.

Tragically, Cruz died of a heart attack on September 2, 2008, while swimming in the pool at his apartment complex in Arizona. He was only 52 years old.

From Skates to Cleats

Did you know two different teams went by the name of the Edmonton Eskimos? Here's the rather twisted and confusing story about it all.

In 1895, Edmonton played its first series of organized games with the formation of the Alberta Rugby Football Union. Two years later, we had a football team called the Esquimaux. In 1910, they officially changed their name to the Edmonton Eskimos.

But there was also another Edmonton Eskimos sports team. They played hockey in the Alberta Amateur Hockey Association, and they challenged for the Stanley Cup in 1910. However, they weren't called the Edmonton Eskimos at that point. In the first half of 1910, they were simply called the Edmonton Hockey Club. In the latter half of 1910, they were the Edmonton Eskimos.

The Edmonton Eskimos hockey team played in the Stanley Cup finals three times but lost each time, though they later won the Western Canada Hockey League championship in the 1922–23 season. The team folded in 1927. Team alumni included Eddie Shore, who went on to become a famous defenceman for the Boston Bruins.

In 1938, the Edmonton Eskimos football team joined the Western Interprovincial Football Union.

The Eskimos that Edmontonians know and love rose to prominence in 1949, wearing their now famous green-and-gold uniforms. One year later, the Eskimos made history, but in a way that had nothing to do with how well they performed. In 1950, they played the Winnipeg Blue Bombers in the first professional football game played at night under lights.

The Edmonton Eskimos football team also made history by winning the Grey Cup more than any other team in the CFL except the Toronto Argonauts. The Eskimo won it 13 times, the Argonauts 16 times.

DID YOU KNOW?

On 92 Street and 93 Avenue, in an otherwise completely average neighbourhood in the city, a house is decked out in green and gold. It's not any kind of "official" home of the Edmonton Eskimos. An Esks fan just decided to paint it that way—to show his Edmonton spirit and all.

AND IN THIS CORNER!

Tiny Boxer

Local boxer Scotty Olson was considered too small for sports when he was a kid. At 1.5 metres tall (that's only 5 feet!), he weighed no more than 55 kilograms. In 1982, when he was 14, Olson met Al Ford, a former Canadian lightweight champion who told him to head to Edmonton's Cougar Boxing Club. At the end of his first lesson, the young man proclaimed that he loved the boxing club and wanted to be the champion of the world. It was that kind of bluster and self-belief that earned him the title of "Bulldog."

His self-confidence more than paid off. In 1984, Bulldog Olson won both the provincial flyweight title and the Canadian championship. Two years later, he won the gold medal at the Commonwealth Games in Edinburgh, Scotland. Two years after that he was representing Canada at the Olympic Games in Seoul, South Korea.

With a record of 34 wins (25 by knockout), it's no wonder Bulldog Olson was inducted into the Alberta Sports Hall of Fame in 2009.

DID YOU KNOW?

In 1988, the notorious boxing celebrity Mike Tyson was supposed to fight here in an event that was to be called "The Weekend of Champions." Tyson pulled out because he had a medical condition (although no one had ever heard of that particular medical condition).

Those who may remember the whole debacle will surely also recall that Tyson's colourful manager Don King referred to us as "Edmonites."

From Football to Wrestling

He once billed himself as "Canada's Greatest Athlete." Whether or not he believed it is a moot point. Eugene Nicholas "Gene" Kiniski just used that mantle for promotional purposes. Born outside of Edmonton, Gene Kiniski went on to become a world champion wrestler. He also became the father of two wrestlers, Nick and Kelly.

Perhaps one of Kiniski's most interesting claims to fame is that he was one of the first World Champion wrestlers to have a background in football. He got his start when Annis Stukus, a scout for the Edmonton Eskimos, took notice of him in 1949.

In the Eskimos training camp he attended, there were other wrestlers too, including Al Oeming and Stu Hart. Stu Hart was the founder of Stampede Wrestling and the father of famous wrestlers Bret and Owen Hart.

DID YOU KNOW?

Al Oeming went on to explore his love of wildlife by starting up a game farm. Many one-time elementary school students in Edmonton and area (like me) remember Al Oeming as the guy who came to their school and talked about animals—with a live cheetah!

HEAVENLY ROLLERS AND THE LITTLE PRINCE

Roller Derby

Whether it's considered a real sport, a symbol of female empowerment or a novelty doesn't matter, frankly. Roller derby is cool. And there's a roller derby league right in St. Albert, just north of Edmonton. The St. Albert Heavenly Rollers (STAHR) Derby League started up in September 2010 with the intention of providing a safe and fun haven for fearless women athletes committed to excellence in sportsmanship.

The Heavenly Rollers are open to women age 18 and up, of any race, creed, colour, background or athletic ability.

Legend of the Birkebeiner

For over two decades, people have been willing to travel great distances to withstand the bitter cold of a western Canadian winter to participate in the Canadian Birkebeiner, Canada's largest cross-country ski festival. The event is held every February just 35 kilometres southeast of Edmonton in the Cooking Lake–Blackfoot Provincial Recreation Area.

This festival has attracted cross-country skiers from all across Canada, the U.S. and as far away as Norway. They are called here by the power of a legend.

That legend began in the year 1206. At the time, Norway was embroiled in a civil war that left the baby prince and heir to the throne, Haakon Haakonsson, in grave danger. When events forced the infant prince into hiding, two brave and hearty warriors travelled over two mountain ranges to rescue him. On their feet they were wearing Birkebeiners (or, in English, footwear made of birch bark). When the warriors carried the young prince home on skis, the prince was crowned, ending the civil war.

Some participants go to great lengths to recreate the legend. One year at the Birkebeiner, 264 men and 35 women travelled the full 55 kilometres of the Birkebeiner course with a five-kilogram pack, to simulate the weight of the baby prince.

Let's Go Wild

Edmonton—a great place to watch wildlife.
And animals.

–Graham Neil, arts reporter, CTV News

FURRY CREATURES

While working on this book, I found myself having numerous "close encounters" with wildlife. One evening, my older brother and I were out walking in the back field of my father's acreage in Ellerslie, just south of Edmonton (although this one-time farming community is now in the city limits). An owl swooped down silently over our heads. I swear it was so close I could look right into its eyes.

A few weeks later, I was out for a stroll with my beloved significant other on a Friday evening. We were startled at dusk by a bird that seemed to be flying strangely, like it was vaguely drunk. When it flew just inches from us, it was obvious that this was no bird. It was a bat.

And just a few weeks later, while staying at a little bed and breakfast north of Edmonton, I looked up from my seat in the dining room and saw two black bears ambling along outside. "Wow!" I said. (Eloquent, huh?) "Bears," I said, near breathless. "Two of them."

The Native woman who owned the bed and breakfast with her husband believed it was a sign. Whether or not my animal encounters meant anything is up for grabs. What I do know is this: open your eyes to the marvels of the natural world and you will see things that make you go "Wow!"

Sasquatch Sightings

Have there been Sasquatch sightings in Edmonton? No, not technically. But Peter Huele, BSc., Live Culture and Natural History Outreach Technician with the Royal Alberta Museum, has some big, weird tales to tell about Bigfoot, Yeti, Wetico or whatever moniker you choose for this hairy, mythical "man-thing."

According to Huele, the respected Canadian explorer David Thompson once talked about a creature like this in his travels across the western Canadian plains. There are also many Cree stories about something called a wetigo (also referred to as a "wendigo"). According to the legend, the wetigo was likely a human being at first, until it was abused by someone—or some-*thing*—and then it became a wild, deranged wetigo lurking through the woods to exact revenge upon its abuser.

There are rumours that once upon a time, people in Alberta were actually hanged on the suspicion of being a wetigo.

"No scientist takes this stuff seriously," Huele admits, "but maybe there's something there. Maybe it was just a way to describe some trapper getting cabin fever. Who knows?"

DID YOU KNOW?

If you happen to glimpse a rare sighting of the porcupine living under one of the buildings at the John Janzen Nature Centre in Edmonton's river valley, rest assured that it won't shoot its quills at you. Porcupines don't shoot their quills. They get rid of them simply by shedding them. The quills protect them against hungry predators, like bears. (Imagine eating food covered with sewing needles! Not so appetizing, is it?)

Strange Cat

Seeing a lynx in the city is rare. But that's precisely what Paul Gregg saw in July 2013...not just once but twice in one day!

Early on a Sunday morning, Gregg caught a glimpse of a lynx coming out of an alley in his Sherbrooke neighbourhood. Later in the day, he saw it again, upon hearing the racket of magpies next to his neighbour's property. When he walked up to a hedge, he realized something was inside the bush, but not for long. As it bolted away, he realized he'd caught his second lynx sighting of the day.

Lynx are incredibly shy of people and rarely found in cities.

Wildlife officers from Fish and Wildlife confirmed another lynx sighting the following Monday, on the grounds of Edmonton's municipal airport downtown.

Even Stranger Cat

Edmonton actor and comedian Dana Anderson is known mostly for *Die-Nasty,* the improvised soap opera that's been playing in the city for over two decades. Anderson might also be known as the guy who saw something he initially called a "fox-cat."

That was how he described the creature to his friends: the animal was a cross between a fox and a cat.

Anderson first saw this "fox-cat" on his family's farm in the hamlet of Rochester, Alberta, which is between Westlock and Athabasca. Although the whole story might seem like a yarn that's the stuff of theatre more than real life, it turns out that such a creature does exist. It's actually called a "fisher."

Fishers weigh up to 10 kilograms, are 1 to 1.2 metres in length, and they've been known to have the attitude of a wolverine (think *fierce*). They exist primarily in the boreal forests of Canada, where they subsist on prey such as mice, squirrels, rabbits, even porcupines. One thing they *don't* eat is fish.

So where did an animal that looks like a cross between fox and a cat get a name like a "fisher"? The name comes from early settlers who thought the animals looked like European polecats, known in France as *fichet*.

"Bertie" Beaver

One of Canada's national symbols happens to be North America's largest rodent: the beaver. Some adult beavers can weigh up to 35 kilograms. "Bertie Beaver," however, weighs much more than that. But his weight varies depending on the person who happens to be *inside* of him that day.

Confused? Don't be. Bertie Beaver is the official mascot of Alberta Environment and Sustainable Resource Development. This truly cuddly mascot was created by Walt Disney in 1958. Bertie was a gift to the people of Alberta in appreciation of the provincial government's support while Disney's film crews were working in Kananaskis Country. The footage shot there was used in Disney's popular TV series *True Life Adventures*.

One of the shows included some of Bertie's family members.

Not mascots.

Real ones.

There *are* real beavers in Edmonton, too. They love the trees surrounding the Whitemud and Blackmud Creeks. In particular, they love chopping down those trees with their substantial and incredibly efficient teeth. The dams they build out of all that wood has a nasty little habit of flooding the ravines and occasionally even causing redirection of the creeks.

DID YOU KNOW?

Edmonton reportedly has no rats. There are no rats in Alberta, period. This isn't by chance. It's because the provincial government has had a program to keep rats out of the city for four decades now. Say what you will about government bureaucracy, but this particular program seems to be working just fine!

There's a Horse in the Walls

Okay, horses aren't exactly "furry," but they have hair. And this is one hair-raising tale shared by an Edmonton woman named Alison Lennie. Actually, it's a story from her father, who explained to her that when he was growing up in Beverly in the city's northeast area in the late 1950s, his friends heard a horse whinnying through the walls of their basement.

Not knowing what else to do, they called the fire department. When the firefighters arrived, one thing led to another until in the end—a *happy* ending, thankfully—a horse was rescued. It had been trapped in the shaft of a coal mine. The Beverley area was indeed built upon many coal mining shafts.

WHAT BUGS YOU?

Creepy Crawlers

They're much smaller than a Sasquatch. In fact, they're usually only about 2.5 centimetres long. But a cutworm sighting is a rare occurrence. During the day, they hide under litter and soil. They typically come out at night, feeding on plants by attacking the stem and cutting it down.

Peter Huele of the Royal Alberta Museum once received a creature so odd that he couldn't identify it at first. After conferring with colleagues, he discovered that it was a species of cutworm caterpillar. Although "cutworm" is their common name, in a strictly biological sense they're actually caterpillars.

Killer Wasps

If you ever happen to see a caterpillar with "horns" anywhere in or around Edmonton, it's likely a Canadian tiger swallowtail caterpillar. The horns, technically called osmeterium, appear when the caterpillar is stressed, as a way of protecting itself (by appearing scary). And there's nothing that can stress out a caterpillar like a wasp. With good reason. According to Peter Huele, Royal Alberta Museum bug room, bees are essentially vegetarians while wasps get their nutrients from nectar and flesh. There are over 60,000 species of wasps in the world that are parasitic. Just one of those species is named *ichneumonidae*. To keep their species alive, they sting other creatures like caterpillars so they can paralyze them and lay their eggs on or inside them.

Remember that scene in the movie *Alien* where the alien pops out of the guy's stomach? Wasps are sort of like the creature in *Alien*. They need a host in order to survive.

Gross, huh?

The Good Side of Parasitic Wasps

Aphids are destructive insects that do a great deal of damage to cultivated plants. So why would horticulturists at the Devonian Botanic Garden have an "aphid farm"? Senior horticulturist Sherrie Benson, who is in charge of the garden's greenhouses, puts cages on select plants with an aphid infestation and then releases parasitic wasps into the cage. The wasps hunt down the aphids and implant their wasp offspring, which feed on their aphid host. This in turn creates more wasps, resulting in an army of anti-aphid warriors.

Adult wasps at Devonian are provided with flowers so they can feed on the nectar and are then released from the "farm" into the greenhouse to hunt down and destroy other aphid infestations.

The Giant Water Bug

One of the weirdest creatures in Edmonton and area has to be the giant water bug. These cockroach-like creatures are identifiable by their pincers and their piercing, sucking mouth parts. They're also notable for their size. One of the largest insects in Alberta, they can grow to as long as 5.5 centimetres (although the one my significant other saw was closer to 7.5 centimetres).

Considering their size and their pincers, giant water bugs may look dangerous, but they're not—at least to humans. With their powerful front legs, they've been known to grab small fish, frogs and salamanders—for the sake of having a meal, no less!

The only time you might run across a giant water bug is in late summer or early fall. That's when the adults leave their shallow ponds at night to find a bigger body of water where they can spend the winter below the ice. One of the ways that giant water bugs search for these larger bodies of water is to watch for something that glows in the night, like the moon glistening on the water surface. They sometimes mistake porch lights and other sources of light for moonlight.

Although they are harmless to humans, if you happen to find one, please remember that one of its nicknames is "toe biter." If you accidentally step on one and it bites you in self-defence, it'll really sting.

The Cyclops Moth

Do you ever get the feeling you're being watched? If so, there might be a polyphemus silk moth somewhere nearby. The moth is as big as the hand of a fully grown human and has an average wingspan of 15 centimetres. Its most notable feature is the big purple markings on its two hind wings. Each of the markings looks like a big eye, which is where it got its name—from the ancient Greek myth of the Cyclops Polyphemus. The markings deter predators.

DID YOU KNOW?

More than 30 species of mosquitoes live in the Edmonton area—and the problem mosquito is called a "vexans mosquito." Because of these troublesome bugs, some summers can be miserable outdoors, especially at dusk.

THINGS WITH WINGS

Mutant Magpie

If you're going for a leisurely stroll in Edmonton and you happen to see from the corner of your eye what appears to be an albino magpie, don't worry that you're losing your mind. There is indeed such a bird as a white magpie. But they're extremely rare. And at least six of them are presumed to be in Edmonton, according to the Royal Alberta Museum.

White magpies aren't actual albinos, although they may appear to be upon first sight. Because unlike true albinos, they have black—not red—eyes, they are said to be "imperfect albinos." White magpies are simply presumed to have a genetic defect that reduces the amount of black pigments in their plumage, making the birds appear more light grey in colour.

It is believed that they have been in Edmonton since at least the 1940s and are descendents of one magpie in which the grey mutation first occurred.

Whitemud Woodpecker

Remember the cartoon character Woody Woodpecker? He was the one with the flaming red crest on his head. "Woody" would be considered a pileated woodpecker, and you can find this bird in Edmonton, generally in the Whitemud Creek Ravine and in the upscale Wolf Willow area.

You will definitely know a pileated woodpecker when you see one. It's big, for starters, nearly the size of a crow. The bird is also beautiful—black with bold white stripes down the neck and that flaming red crest on its head.

You will also know one by *hearing* it. Pileated woodpeckers whack at dead trees with their beaks in search of their favourite food—carpenter ants. When they're not knocking on wood, they're also known to make a sound that's a bit like monkeys, believe it or not.

Owl Attack

In November 2011, Darrell Bablitz and his wife Roxcanna Porenchuk of Edmonton reported that when they let out their one-year-old Yorkshire terrier Maggie May into their backyard, out of the blue, the dog was attacked—and killed—by a snowy owl.

Snowy owls spend their summers in their natural habitat of the Canadian tundra. During the winter months they can be found in large cities like Edmonton, but sightings are rare—and reports of them attacking pets are rarer yet.

Like all owls, they are definitely master hunters. One advantage in hunting is an owl's ability to turn its head all the way around on its neck. Owls can't move their eyeballs the way we can, and they don't have peripheral vision, so moving their head allows them to see. Another advantage in their hunting style is that they are utterly silent when they fly—you can't hear the flapping of their wings.

DID YOU KNOW?

The northern saw-whet owl has feathered claws. This species of owl stays here in the winter so the soft, plush feathers help to keep the owl's clawed feet warm during our standard sub-zero temperatures.

Birds That Stay Home

Let's face it: if you had wings and you could fly somewhere warm for Edmonton's famously chilly winter months, you'd do it without thinking. Blue jays are different. They're like that person who doesn't go out on a Friday or Saturday night and prefers to stay home watching a DVD.

Blue jays are able to survive our cold winter months because they're smart. Throughout the year, they hide little caches of food in numerous places. And they remember where they've stored those caches. They place them near landmarks, such as tall trees.

Cute But Tough

Chickadees also spend their winters here. It's because they're tough. These cute and tiny feathered friends are resilient enough to stick around during even the coldest of Edmonton winters, in temperatures as low as or lower than –40°C. One of their tricks to lasting the winter is their choice of real estate. They stay among the boughs of spruce trees and stick closer to the centre of the tree, where it's warmer.

Chickadees are also friendly—especially in winter, when they're hungry. Put some bird seed in your hand, stand completely still, try not to make a peep and you might literally have a chickadee eating out of the palm of your hand.

PLANT IT

The definition of "flora" is "plants considered as a group, especially the plants of a particular country, region or time." The country is Canada, the region is "weird Edmonton" and for the time, well, hopefully these beautiful, odd and even tasty examples of local plant life will be here for a long time indeed.

Foul Flower

What's hairy, purple-red, shaped like a starfish and smells awful? It's the carrion flower, a stinky flower from the plant *Stapelia hirsuta*, which can be found blooming in the Arid Showhouse at the Devonian Botanic Garden in late fall and early spring. The flower smells like a dead animal, which is precisely what flies like best. Tricked into landing on the flower to lay their eggs, flies and carrion beetles pollinate the plant.

In other words, if it didn't reek, its species couldn't survive.

Another Putrid Flower

On April 21, 2013, in one of the glass pyramids of Edmonton's Muttart Conservatory, the tallest flower in the world started to bloom. It also started to stink. Really, really stink. Some people said the putrid odour smelled like rotting meat. Others claimed it was worse—more like rotting diapers.

The name of this giant flower is, fittingly, Putrella, from the species *Amorphophallus titanum*. Its more common nickname is even more fitting: the corpse flower. Originally found in the jungles of Sumatra, the corpse flower in the Muttart Conservatory was believed to be the first of its kind to bloom in western Canada.

And it bloomed quickly. In just over one month, it went from a bud 2 centimetres high to a giant flower over 2 metres tall.

The corpse flower stinks for the same reason as the *Stapelia hirsuta*. It attracts the flies required for pollination.

The Century Plant

Another miraculous plant found in the glass pyramids of the Muttart Conservatory is the *Agave americana*, more commonly known as "the century plant." In the summer of 2013, in the course of just a few months, it sprouted from almost one metre high to more than 9 metres, almost reaching the top of the pyramid.

It also began to bloom, for the first—and final—time in 35 years.

The century plant lives to bloom and then blooms to die. In other words, the brilliant green-yellow flowers it began to sprout that summer signalled its demise.

This particular plant first came to the Muttart Conservatory in 1977 as a 45-centimetre plant in a simple 8-litre pot. It grew to be so beloved by staff that it was given a nickname of "Beila."

There's a happy ending to Beila's saga. At Beila's base were three little baby century plants.

Cattails or Hot Dogs?

In the spring, you can eat the cattails that grow in Edmonton's ponds. You have to eat them in spring, though, when they are greenish, not brown. You could eat them raw, but they taste better barbecued, which only makes sense, since they *look* like a wiener. You can also eat the root of the cattail. It has a taste akin to asparagus.

Tea Time

Pineapple weed grows all over the city. You'll recognize it by its flowers, which are tiny, round, yellow-green and soft. Bend down, pluck off one of the flowers, pinch it between your thumb and forefinger, roll it around a bit and take a sniff. Right away, you'll discover that pineapple weed is aptly named. It gives off a pineapple smell when it's crushed.

You can pick these bulbous yellow-green flower heads and make tea out of them. It tastes like chamomile and is similarly relaxing.

Don't Eat the Black Spruce

Only two types of spruce grow naturally in Edmonton: white spruce and black spruce. A white spruce looks like a Christmas tree—full at the bottom and tapering off to a point at the top. A black spruce doesn't look like a Christmas tree at all, even barely like a Charlie Brown Christmas tree! To first lay your eyes on a black spruce you might think the tree is dying or dead.

If you're out with a date on a trail and you don't have any breath mints, find a white spruce, pinch off a needle, put it in your mouth and suck on it for a few seconds. Your mouth will come alive with a pine-flavoured, amazingly refreshing and almost minty quality.

Don't try this with a black spruce. Because black spruce trees generally grow in more acidic soils—usually in bogs—their needles are distinctly bitter tasting.

That's putting it lightly. They taste a little like cat pee—or so I've heard.

Whispers in the Wind

We have aspen trees in Edmonton and area. One of the most beautiful aspens is the trembling aspen. They're the trees that make that especially calming sound of a breeze rustling through the leaves. The leaves' flattened stems are designed in such a way that they really "jiggle" in the breeze.

Here's another neat fact about the trembling aspen: they wear their own form of sunscreen. Run the palm of your hand over the trunk of a trembling aspen and look down at your palm. You will see that it's coated with a soft, white, powder-like substance. Trembling aspens produce this thin layer to protect their greenish bark from the sun and to ensure that the tree retains its nutrients through the winter months.

Perhaps the best place to see aspens is Elk Island National Park. This aspen parkland is less than an hour northeast of Edmonton. Trees aren't the park's only draw. Elk Island is considered second only to Africa's famous Serengeti for wildlife viewing. It has the second highest density of hoofed animals per square kilometre in the entire world. By "hoofed" animals, I mean moose, elk and free-roaming herds of bison.

No Nightmare on Elm Street

Edmonton is home to North America's largest urban forest of elms. With more than 60,000, the city also has the largest population of Dutch elm disease-free trees in the world—and we're working hard to keep it that way. Numerous groups help the city monitor the magnificent elms, and disease prevention efforts are in place to keep our elms alive and healthy.

Who Loves Lichen?

Lichen is considered both a moss and a fungus. It's also ancient, outdating the dinosaurs. And over time, lichen can do the most amazing feats. When they cling to boulders, they can eventually—over centuries—break that boulder down until it becomes soil.

A type of lichen called "old man's beard lichen" can be found in Edmonton and area. Strangely, this type of lichen was once used to stimulate hair growth.

This Tree Really Parties

If ever in autumn you notice birds that seem, well, drunk, they've probably been sampling the bright red berries that grow in bunches on mountain ash trees. In fall, these berries ferment. The taste might be irresistible to the birds, but if they eat too many of the berries, they will definitely become a little dazed. If you have a mountain ash tree in your yard, protect your windows (and the birds) by applying a few cardboard silhouettes of birds to the glass. This will keep the inebriated birds from flying toward your home.

As an additional note, the berries from mountain ash trees are edible for humans too. They taste a little like cranberries but with a slightly bitter flavour. To make the berries more palatable, wait until the first frost to pick and eat the mountain ash berries. The frost makes the berries sweeter.

Eat Me

Edible plants grow practically under the noses of Edmontonians. Here are just a few:

- The berries from dwarf dogwood plants are edible. They taste like apples. But it's the plants they come from that are particularly "weird." They disperse their pollen with a force 800 times stronger than the force that astronauts use during liftoff.
- Labrador tea is a common evergreen shrub. The leaves can be used medicinally to treat colds, heartburn and hangovers.
- Speaking of tea, purple avens can be found in the marshes and swamps in the Edmonton area. Boil the roots for 10 to 15 minutes, add some sugar and milk and you'll have a tea that tastes a bit like hot chocolate.

Common Plants, Uncommon Uses

Other plants in the Edmonton area have some beneficial uses:

- Common horsetails have the ability to absorb and accumulate gold and were widely used by prospectors as a means to find gold deposits.
- Curled dock is a common plant with medicinal uses, including the prevention of skin diseases. Mashing the leaves and making a paste relieves the pain of stinging nestles.

MISCELLANEOUS MARVELS

Right Under Our Noses

Here are some truly strange facts about various amphibians, insects and dinosaurs (yes, dinosaurs) found in Edmonton and area…

- Wood frogs freeze solid over winter and thaw again in spring. Northern leopard frogs will eat almost anything that fits into their mouths. They simply sit and wait for something to come by so they can eat it.
- Tiger salamanders are found in any wetland area near Edmonton. They can grow up to 30 centimetres long. And they can eat small mice!
- The mayfly is an ancient and still-living insect related to dragonflies and damselflies. Once they reach adulthood, they don't eat anything at all. There's no time to. Because of their short lifespan, the adults just mate and then die. Mayflies are found near water sources, which is where they lay their eggs.
- There is a dinosaur bone bed in southwest Edmonton. It was a feeding ground for the *Daspletosaurus*, a direct ancestor of *Tyrannosaurus Rex*. It is also the bone bed of *Edmontosaurus*, a duck-billed dinosaur that was first discovered in the late 1800s, allegedly found when a man walking a dog noticed a bone sticking out the side of a creek bed. *Edmontosaurus* can now be found in the Dinosaur Trail at the Royal Tyrell Museum in Drumheller.

Unlucky Elephant

For 35 years now, Edmonton has been home to a lone elephant named Lucy. But if you ask at least one animal rights group calling itself "Save Lucy," this is no home at all. Our winters are cold, for starters. Elephants, and particularly female elephants, need a moderate climate, large spaces to roam and other elephants with which to socialize.

Edmonton's Valley Zoo provides none of those things, the members of Save Lucy argue, adding that Lucy's small and barren enclosure offers no room for others of her species. Valley Zoo spokespeople have said that Lucy has grown accustomed to the city's climate and should not be moved.

In April 2012 the Supreme Court of Canada refused the case of this unlucky elephant. In November of that year, Lucy got national coverage when the CBC-TV news program *The Fifth Estate* ran a story on her plight.

When in October 2013 the Toronto Zoo transported its three elephants to a more appropriate sanctuary in California, members of Save Lucy held a protest at the Valley Zoo, demanding that Lucy be reassessed to see if it would be safe to move her.

At present, Lucy remains in captivity.

DID YOU KNOW?

Garter snakes, native to Edmonton and area, are venomous but not to humans. They also hibernate in the winter. One metre under the ground, they stay in a new accommodation known as a "hibernaculum."

Festival City

We're a theatre/sports town. The percentage of the population that goes to the theatre is nothing of what goes to the hockey games, but the level of commitment and sophistication of that theatre-going audience is great.

–Bob Baker, former artistic director
of Citadel Theatre

LET US ENTERTAIN YOU

There is one good reason why Edmonton is known as Canada's Festival City.

Actually, no, scratch that. There are more than 30 reasons why, back in 2001, Edmonton became one of the first cities anywhere to create a centralized office to organize and support its festivals. Each year more than 30 festivals take place in Edmonton. Some of them are big. Some of them are small. And some of them are just plain weird.

On the surface, Edmonton might seem like a relatively normal city. But it's not. It's a place where people celebrate life in sometimes bizarre ways.

Bring Your Own Fringe

The Edmonton International Fringe Festival began in 1982 and is now considered the second largest Fringe theatre festival in the world, just shy of the famous Edinburgh Festival Fringe. Every year in mid-August, our festival attracts 600,000 visitors to the Old Strathcona district, to take in more than 1000 theatrical performances and a wide array of street performers. But it's not Edmonton's size and popularity that makes the Fringe so great. Our city's Fringe has a way of making the arts even a bit, well, artsier.

One of the aspects making the Fringe Festival bigger and bigger each year is its penchant for BYOVs, or Bring Your Own Venue. A number of Fringe Festivals across North America use the term "BYOV," but it was first coined in Edmonton. The original concept for a BYOV was that it worked particularly well if the play

was site specific. For example, if the play takes place in a restaurant, don't do it in a theatre—perform the play in a restaurant.

BYOVs started at the Edmonton Fringe in 1992. One of the festival's BYOV plays was *A Midsummer Night's Ice Dream* by The National Ice Theatre of Canada. The play was held at the Granite Curling Club.

Another interesting example of a BYOV is *Dead Slow,* which took place in 1993 at the Renford Inn On Whyte (which is now the Varscona Hotel). The play wasn't held in a room at the inn. It took place at the hotel's parking garage. The plot focused on a serial killer who only preys on prominent TV anchormen. It had a seedy feel to it, reminiscent of *All the President's Men,* when journalists Woodward and Bernstein meet their source Deep Throat in parking garages. The actors in *Dead Slow* arrived in cars, got out, did their scenes and then at the end of the play, they simply drove away.

Another example of a BYOV—and a weird one at that—is *Steel Kiss*, which also made its debut in 1993. The play was set in a park. Traditional BYOV logic would dictate that you find a park, set up a bunch of chairs and perform the play there, but the play's director had something different in mind. He found a popular Whyte Avenue night club, the now defunct Rebar, and somehow convinced the managers to lay sod on the floor so that when the audience came to see this indoor show, they could have the sensation of being outside, by sitting on the grass.

The BYOV concept is continuing to grow at the Edmonton Fringe. In their first year, there were three BYOVs. In 2013, there were 41 BYOV locations.

Fringe Follower

In 1992, movie star Elliott Gould (who would later play Ross and Monica's dad on *Friends*) was appearing at a dinner theatre play at Edmonton's Mayfield Inn, on the west side. But even he could not resist the allure of the Fringe, which was taking place a good 20-minute drive from the hotel. Gould not only attended a few shows, but he also read stories to children in a tent at the KidsFringe.

DID YOU KNOW?

Early in his career, Bruce McCulloch of *Kids in the Hall* fame did a one-man show at the 1986 Edmonton Fringe. Called *Trapped on a Lawnchair*, the event used movement and music as a surreal backdrop to McCulloch's true suburban stories—like the one about the time his dad lost his teeth to a goose.

Fun with "Found" Art

Another arts festival in Edmonton takes the Edmonton Fringe Festival's Bring Your Own Venue concept to its zenith. It's called the Found Festival. Absolutely all of the festival's performances are held in unconventional locations. One theatre piece was performed inside a parked car on the street (and to see it, you simply had to crowd around the vehicle). Another performance, a solo musical act, took place on top of a dumpster in a back alley.

One of the weirdest aspects about the Found Festival is that if you're walking around Old Strathcona's Whyte Avenue during the last weekend of June, you could likely come across it by accident. At first, you're probably not going to be sure if it's a performance or real life. The whole idea of this kind of art is that it's supposed to be a surprise and challenge you.

The Found Festival started up in 2009 because its organizers recognized that, in order to be seen, artists need to have a space in which to perform or display their art. For visual artists in particular, that's difficult, especially if you're a young emerging artist. Renting a gallery space isn't easy when you're not flush with cash. So the Found Festival's philosophy is to empower young artists by saying, "You *can* showcase your art. Do it. Almost anywhere."

This whole pseudo guerrilla art concept is growing in Edmonton, thanks to the Found Festival. Others are taking the idea and running with it in some unique ways. Thou Art Here Theatre finds fascinating ways to make the works of William Shakespeare a little more contemporary, such as performing the Bard's greatest drinking scenes in different bars around town.

What's next? Arriving at your house or apartment, opening the door and finding someone else's play happening in your bathroom? Don't knock it. Maybe we're not that far off.

Forget Paris

Paris might be considered one of the most romantic cities in the world, but face it, do you really want to visit the City of Light during the height of the tourist season? Instead, why not spend one weekend in the middle of July feeling like you're in Paris when in fact you're in Edmonton?

The Whyte Avenue Art Walk Festival has been compared to being "sort of like the Left Bank of Paris." For three days every July, this festival transforms one of the funkiest shopping districts of Edmonton into a big outdoor studio and gallery. Everywhere you look for a full stretch of 4 kilometres, you can see the original works of over 400 working artists on display, and practically every kind of art medium and subject imaginable: oil paintings, pastels, nature stuff, super wild surrealism, even graffiti-style street art on canvas.

Sometimes the art of it all can't be contained on canvas. For years, one of the biggest attractions of the Art Walk Festival has been a man named Daniel Anderson, who becomes a living sculpture. He dresses up as a white canvas, and people can draw and paint on him.

DID YOU KNOW?

The Old Strathcona district has a festival that features Canada's best Francophone musical acts. It's called the Edmonton Chante Festival, and it takes place at the end of September. In order to keep a distinctly European flavour to the proceedings, the festival's organizers handpick venues with good French food and wine.

Winter Wonderland

One of the most iconic festivals Edmonton has to offer is the Ice on Whyte Festival and its International Ice Carving Competition. That's because the festival takes place at the pinnacle of winter, in January. Since 2003, this festival has been turning the city into a truly magical winter wonderland.

Walk through the End of Steel Park in Old Strathcona, just north of Whyte Avenue—hence "Ice on Whyte"—and you'll see magnificent ice sculptures, such as a life-sized lion or a finely detailed giant praying mantis. Other ice sculptures made by teams from faraway places such as the Netherlands, Armenia or Russia are so artful and abstract they're indescribable, but stunning all the same.

Making ice sculptures as delicate as blown glass has its drawbacks, according to Wanda Bornn, executive director of Ice on Whyte and its summer cousin Sand on Whyte (see the next entry). "In the very first year we hosted the International Ice Carving Competition, the weather suddenly warmed up," she says. "An ice castle started as a great big piece of amazing work, but soon enough people were placing bets on when it would come crashing down. The judges of the competition had to madly judge the sculptures to beat the melting!

"In Europe, castles stand for centuries," she muses, "but here they only last four days!"

Bornn has always found it incredible how many people will come to Ice on Whyte even when the weather swings in the opposite direction. "People come out in minus 40 degrees Celsius to see the sculptures and play on the giant ice slide or do Frozen Karaoke. It's amazing," she says.

Equally amazing was the 3-metre-high fire-and-ice chimney the festival had in 2012. On a frosty winter day, a huge crowd gathered around the crackling flames to watch as the "ice" part of the chimney slowly started to dissolve.

And, yes, in the end, it all came crashing down. To great cheers and "woos," of course!

Whyte Avenue Beach Party

If you think working with ice sounds tricky, try making a sculpture out of sand. That's the thrill behind a new summer festival

on Whyte Avenue known as "Sand on Whyte." Held in conjunction with Whyte Avenue's Art Walk event in mid-July, Sand on Whyte is a summertime version of Ice on Whyte, this time featuring massive sculptures made from sand mixed with water.

The sand comes from a creek bed near Camrose, about 75 kilometres east of Edmonton. Fortunately, the sand contains enough clay to make it a little easier to work with. That said, it's not a rarity to see a piece of a creation fall off mid-sculpting. Somehow, sand sculptors don't blink an eye over such losses. They view their work as "performance art"—battling the elements is just part of the fun.

According to Wanda Bornn, the ultimate vision for this festival would be to put on a "beach party" every summer, complete with beach volleyball.

Return of the Squeezebox

It took a nosedive in popularity after the advent of Elvis and The Beatles, but some say it's starting to make a comeback.

The accordion, that is.

In Edmonton, a small but passionate group of accordion fans have put together the Accordion Extravaganza Festival, and the three-day event does indeed seem to have its audience. The festival has taken place for not one but almost 20 years now, every September. And these squeezebox fans aren't alone. Across North America, in places such as the famous Knott's Berry Farm, accordion festivals have been all the rage.

One popular accordion group is the Ulster Accordion Band, which has played at the Disney World Christmas Parade, the King Orange Bowl Parade in Florida, and Edmonton's Accordion Extravaganza Festival, of course.

A highlight of the festival, aside from the performances, is the accordion competition. People ranging from six-year-old kids to seniors well into their 80s enter the competition. The musical styles covered are every bit as varied, too, from polkas to classical. (What? No punk rock or heavy metal?)

By the way, if you're thinking of taking up the accordion and entering in the competition one of these years, here's something to think about: the accordion can be played anywhere, sitting around the campfire or on the bus. You sure can't do that with a piano!

The Fountain of Youth

Think of it as a Fringe Theatre Festival for seniors. That's probably the best way to describe one of Edmonton's most interesting and revolutionary arts festivals, the Creative Age Festival.

First held in 2008, this festival encourages seniors to gain hands-on experience with the arts through workshops in drama, music, dance, as well as visual and literary arts. The philosophy is that in the process of losing themselves in the arts, seniors will feel younger and more vibrant...sort of like taking a dip in the fountain of youth.

The Creative Age Festival also puts bums in seats, as the showbiz saying goes. Many of the performances focus on issues related to aging—and to ensure they ring true, the actors themselves are seniors. There have been plays about Alzheimer's disease and about death and dying. If that sounds a tad dark, a lot of light and levity is part of the festival too, including an octogenarian stand-up comic.

The festival takes its cue from some of the amazing work done by the National Center for Creative Aging (in the U.S.) and the groundbreaking research completed by the late American psychiatrist Gene Cohen.

Some impressive research into creative aging is happening here in Edmonton, too. The University of Alberta is completing a sociological study called "Theatre as a Pathway to Healthy Aging." One of the key people involved in that study is David Barnet, a professor in the Department of Drama at the University of Alberta.

Barnet is also the brainchild behind GeriActors and Friends, the theatre group that has performed plays and hosted workshops for the Creative Age Festival. Made up of 12 seniors, seven graduate students and undergrads, this troupe breaks down barriers. They get up and sing rock and roll. They're learning to do improv comedy. They even do outreach with a local high school theatre class.

DID YOU KNOW?

To say that the work done by GeriActors and Friends is liberating would be an understatement. One of the actresses involved had a lifelong ambition of playing Juliet in William Shakespeare's *Romeo and Juliet*. Through GeriActors she got her chance in

January 2005. She passed away shortly afterwards, at the age of 84. What's important is that she had lived long enough to realize her dream.

Belly Laughs

You never know what's going to happen during an improv comedy sketch. Sometimes it all ends up with people getting cold gravy dumped on their heads.

Or at least that's been the case at Improvaganza, hosted by Edmonton's acclaimed improv group, Rapid Fire Theatre. For 10 days at the end of June, the Varscona Theatre and other spaces in the Old Strathcona area become the ultimate meeting place for comedy improvisers from across Canada, North America and beyond.

What happens onstage is always, always a surprise. There are Theatresports matches, fake radio shows and people putting jam in their armpits. Seriously.

Well, *not* seriously, actually. This stuff is gut-splitting.

True to the nature of improv comedy, nothing is pre-scripted about the thoroughly inane acts you'll see onstage at Improvaganza. Case in point: Dim Sum. That was the name of the piece performed by the improv troupe Dad's Garage, from Atlanta, Georgia in 2011.

A spoof on one of those outrageous Japanese game shows, Dim Sum put together two teams of unsuspecting improvisers and ran them through a series of strange improv comedy challenges. In each round, the audience voted for the team they liked the best. The results never worked out so well for the losers, however. Instead, bizarre punishments were inflicted upon them, including a kubasa interrogation and doing a shot of vodka with wasabi in it. And yes, it's true. They inevitably ended up with cold gravy dumped on their heads.

Send in the Clowns

Every summer, there comes a time when downtown Edmonton is overrun with clowns. Literally. And it's not just clowns taking the place over. It's also the usual circus-type fair of weirdos: jugglers, acrobats, unicyclists, contortionists, cartoonists, musicians, dancers and other rather loony ilk.

The Edmonton International Street Performers Festival is Canada's first street theatre festival, born in 1985. Every day from 11:00 AM to 11:00 PM for a stretch of 10 days in early July, the city's Sir Winston Churchill Square is transformed into a hilariously fantastical place packed with a host of international and local street artists. All told, this gaggle of gleeful goons delivers over 1500 different outdoor performances.

Besides the great entertainment, the best part, especially for families with young kids and tight budgets, is that the performances are all pay-what-you-can.

Here's the weirdest part: some of these performances get pretty "out there." Expect to see everything from Latin-dancing clowns to a juggler tossing chairs to flaming acrobats (literally with *fire!*).

One year, there was even an interactive experience called "The Silent Disco"—sort of like a scene from that 1977 movie *Saturday Night Fever*, but with the sound off. No music. And the actors stayed silent. The audience, however, found it impossible to keep the volume down on its laughter.

These Bards Mean Business

"The lit industry is becoming sexy," says Rayanne Doucet, executive director of the Edmonton Poetry Festival, which began in 2006 (and by "lit" she means "literature"). "Ten years ago, it was documentary films. Now, books are sexy. Poetry and non-fiction are *especially* sexy."

Spoken-word poetry is growing in popularity, thanks in part to rap music. And, by the way, according to Doucet, "rap" is actually an acronym for "rhythm and poetry." Young people find spoken-word poetry appealing because they don't have to sit and read it; they can just listen to it.

Some of what you hear at the Edmonton Poetry Festival can get sexy indeed. In 2013, George Elliot Clarke, Toronto's poet laureate until 2015, read a saucy piece. "It was very pornographic," explains Doucet. "Plus, he delivers every poem with that big, booming voice. When he speaks, you listen."

Sometimes, the events hosted by the Edmonton Poetry Festival in their various venues (most often downtown) can get all-out bizarre. Take, for example, a poetry reading called *Bling on the Blinks*, put on by an Edmonton arts group called the Stroll of Poets Society. "Blink poetry" is based on the notion that "If you blink, you'll miss it." At this event in 2013, a total of 70 poets were each given 60 seconds to recite their original works. If they went over the time limit, they were gonged and hauled off the stage.

Even weirder is that the event was hosted by a man—local spoken-word artist John Leppard—who wore a dress and a tiara. The latter was his "bling," of course.

You can catch the weirdness—and the sexiness—of the Edmonton Poetry Festival every year in the last week of April, which incidentally is National Poetry Month.

Lights, Camera, Action!

Edmonton loves movies—and movie people love the city right back! Some of the film directors that have come here include John Waters (of *Hairspray* and *Pink Flamingos* infamy), Werner Herzog (known for *Grizzly Man*), Deepa Mehta (director of *Water*) and Norman Jewison (director of *Jesus Christ Superstar* and *Moonstruck*).

What brought them here? West Edmonton Mall? An Oilers game? No. Year after year, acclaimed film directors have travelled here to attend the Edmonton International Film Festival. One of the things they like most about the event, according to the festival's executive director Kerrie Long, is the down-to-earth vibe. Instead of placing the directors on pedestals (or the obligatory director's chair), Long and crew ensure that directors engage in Q & A with Edmonton film fans. They've even gone out for beers afterwards.

The festival is also known for retaining its share of deeply loyal fans. Some of them have stepped up and volunteered for the festival—like Brad Smilanach, an assistant principal teaching film studies at Lillian Osborne High School in Edmonton's Riverbend area. In his first year, his volunteer job on the programming committee came with what he considered to be the ultimate job description—watching movies.

DID YOU KNOW?

Edmonton's Garneau Theatre is home to western Canada's premier horror, cult and sci-fi film fest. It's aptly called DEDFest. So far, the festival, which began in 2007, has unleashed quite the assault of gore on its "DED-heads." The film titles say it all: *The ABCs of Death*, *I Sell the Dead* and *John Dies at the End*.

Do you see a bit of a theme at work here?

Okay, so DEDFest isn't subtle. It's pretty darn cool, though.

COOL CULTURE

Truly World Class

Canada is getting more multicultural. If you want to see a profound example of a new kind of Canadian spirit, head into Edmonton's beautiful river valley on each day of the August long weekend and take a walk through the equally gorgeous Hawrelak Park. What you'll find is a sensation of the sights, sounds, tastes and aromas of more than 85 cultures. It's probably the most profound (and truly enjoyable) way to see the diversity that makes up this western Canadian city.

Up and running since 1975, the Servus Heritage Festival is Canada's longest-established multicultural celebration. It's also one of the biggest. In both 1991 and 1992, the festival hit its attendance record when more than 290,000 people showed up to celebrate. That record was beaten in 2012 when attendance was recorded at over 350,000 people.

A lot of the people who flock to the Heritage Festival are from Edmonton and area, but the event is more than gathering a name for itself internationally. In 1999, the American Bus Association, the trade organization of the motor coach tour industry, designated the festival as one of the Top 100 Events in North America.

Elvis the Beaver?

One of the weirder aspects about the Servus Heritage Festival is that its mascot doesn't seem multicultural, though he is definitely Canadian!

He's called "Buddy the Beaver." Before the mascot first came into existence in 1991, the festival's organizers were having a hard time picking a name for him. Some of the monikers thrown around included Bucky, Beno, Beulah, even Elvis. In the end, the name "Buddy" was chosen by the public in a name-the-mascot contest.

It makes you wonder what would have happened if the Heritage Festival had a mascot named Elvis the Beaver.

Alberta Idol?

In these days of *American Idol* and our own *Canadian Idol*, it's quite common to see up-and-coming vocal talents winning their moment of glory, or what Andy Warhol once called their "15 minutes of fame." Long before the existence of these TV shows, an Edmonton politician was able to achieve his own celebrity status.

To many Edmontonians, Gene Zwozdesky may be generally known for his longstanding contributions as Speaker of the Legislative Assembly of Alberta and a minister of various provincial government departments over the years. But in 1982, he also wrote original music and lyrics for a song called "Then and When," a song-and-dance revue that premiered at the gala for the Heritage Festival.

For several years in the 1980s, the Honourable Gene Zwozdesky served on the festival's board of directors.

Did he go on to a big recording career? No, but he won numerous awards from cultural and arts organizations for his work as a politician...so he's sort of a Government-of-Alberta Idol.

Saved by Volunteers

The Heritage Festival was almost one of the casualties of Edmonton's infamous "Black Friday" tornado on July 31, 1987. The storm struck while the festival was being set up in Hawrelak Park. Strong winds, torrential rains and a violent pelting of hailstones severely damaged most of the tents used for the pavilions and put the fate of the festival in peril.

The festival was saved by group of generous volunteers from different cultural organizations who met at the festival site and went from one tent to another, repairing the damage caused by the storm.

The weather continued to be less than friendly during that August long weekend. At the time, Black Friday had heightened the public's fear of another tornado touching down. Although attendance at the outdoor Heritage Festival was lower that summer, a total of 140,000 people still came out to celebrate.

COWBOY CULTURE

Wild West

As if to remind everyone that we were part of the "wild west"—and maybe we still are—one of Edmonton's best-attended festivals has nothing whatsoever to do with the arts. It's called the Canadian Finals Rodeo, and the name says it all.

Every year in November, almost 100,000 rodeo fans flock to Rexall Place to sit on the edge of their seats as dozens of cowboys compete for the $1-million-plus prize purse, one of the largest in Canadian rodeo.

With Canadian Finals Rodeo action, spectators never know exactly what they're going to get…but then again, sometimes the cowboys don't, either. For the Bull Riding, Bareback and Saddle Bronc event, for example, a contestant's name is drawn out of a hat. More importantly, out of another hat, the name of an animal is also drawn.

In other words, the rider doesn't get to choose the animal he will ride. Every year since the Canadian Finals Rodeo's start in 1974, some animals strike panic and fear into the hearts of even the most rugged cowboy.

The flip side to panic and fear, however, is a little something called adrenaline. And it's powerful stuff. When the matchups of cowboy and animal get pulled from their respective hats, the adrenaline gets pumping. Hard.

DID YOU KNOW?

Edmonton has another festival called the Interstellar Rodeo. The name is a tad misleading, though. Held each late July in the Heritage Amphitheatre in Hawrelak Park, the Interstellar Rodeo has nothing to do with snorting broncos or lassos (or anything "interstellar" for that matter). It does feature mavericks and outlaws, however, only of a musical kind. Some of the acts that have graced the stage of this event include country rock rebels Steve Earle and Kurt Vile, indie faves Serena Ryder and Sarah Harmer and Canada's own Blue Rodeo.

Spectacular Sites

Edmonton has five seasons. Summer, autumn, winter, spring and pothole.

–Marty Chan, Edmonton author

BUILDINGS AND LANDMARKS

Egypt has the Great Pyramids. Paris has the Eiffel Tower. In Alberta, Vegreville has the world's largest Easter egg, St. Paul has the world's first UFO landing pad and everyone knows that the Town of Vulcan has a Spaceship Information Centre and a serious obsession with Star Trek. (Its tourist information centre is called the Vulcan Tourism and Trek Station. Oh, and Leonard Nimoy, the actor who played the famous Vulcan, Mr. Spock, even paid a visit to this small Alberta town back in April 2010.)

Let's face it: landmarks help to put a city on the map.

Edmonton might not have any of the Seven Wonders of the World. And it may not be able to lay any claim to being the lost Atlantis. And we don't have any Lemurians (that we know of). But that doesn't mean it can't be wondrously odd.

Bra Bridge

We've all heard of a drawbridge, but how about a "bra bridge"? Every year at the end of October, the Edmonton radio station 91.7 The Bounce strings bras across the High Level Bridge. It is done for more than a lark (or publicity). The station does it to raise awareness for breast cancer research. October is Breast Cancer Awareness Month.

Built in 1913, Edmonton's High Level Bridge was the first bridge in Canada to accommodate four different kinds of transportation: rail, streetcar, automobile/horse and pedestrian. (You won't see many horses on it these days, however.)

It was constructed with steel and concrete technology that came from the United States—Chicago, to be exact. Made of almost 8000 tonnes of steel that was painted black, it stood 15 storeys high above the North Saskatchewan River and spanned 755 metres from one side of the river to the other.

Today, the one-way High Level Bridge is simply one of the routes that motorists on the north side of the river take in order to get to work, run errands or do some shopping on Whyte Avenue. And the bridge is used a lot. Approximately 30,000 vehicles cross it every day.

As drivers rush about their daily duties, however, does anyone behind the wheel ever pause to think about what this landmark reveals about the history of Edmonton? Likely not. Most Edmontonians don't know that the High Level Bridge was opened in 1913, one year after Edmonton and Strathcona merged as one city. At the time, this bridge was a symbol of the amalgamation of these two separate communities. You could say, in hindsight, that it spoke of the strength that exists in unity.

And it stands strong to this day.

Take a ride on the streetcar on top of the bridge when it's in operation from the May long weekend to Thanksgiving, and you'll get one of the most spectacular views of Edmonton.

Bunker Business

There was a time when Cold War tensions were so high that Edmonton had a top secret bunker. But it's a secret no longer. The bunker is behind a chain-link fence on the north side of Crestwood's McKenzie Ravine, one metre underground, beneath a small concrete shed. Built in 1954, the bunker was sealed up in the 1970s. Now, museum officials are restoring the bunker for a re-opening in 2015.

The west end was chosen as the location for the bunker because it was considered the place to be in the case of a nuclear attack by the Soviets. "It was believed that if the City of Edmonton were to get bombed that it would be in downtown," says Fred Armbruster, executive director of the Edmonton Civil Defense Museum. "By the time the shock would have got over to the west-end, it would be dissipating and this would basically be a safe zone."

Historical resources consultant Ken Tingley was part of a small group that entered the bunker in 2006. "It looks like being in a submarine," he says. "This is quite a depressing hole in the ground." Amazingly, this one-floor concrete box measuring 10 metres by 13 metres was built to fit 36 people, even though they would obviously feel like tightly packed sardines in there.

The Edmonton Historical Board is urging the City of Edmonton to add the bunker to its roster of historic resources.

Grain Elevators

Joseph Dart, a merchant, and Robert Dunbar, an engineer, invented the first grain elevators as a means of storing grain. That was in Buffalo, New York, in 1842, when the city of Edmonton was still a good half a century away from existing. A time came, however, when the landscape of the entire province was dotted with grain elevators, back when agriculture was the primary economic driver. As many as 1733 grain elevators were standing in their heyday. By 2011, only 154 were left.

Perhaps one of the most impressive grain elevators was the massive Ellerslie grain elevator, just south of Edmonton on what was then Highway 2 (now called Queen Elizabeth II Highway). Originally constructed in 1962, the Ellerslie grain elevator gained fame for being one of the tallest structures in the area. It was known by all who passed it for the Bible verse painted upon one side: "For what shall it profit a man, if he shall gain the whole world, and lose his own soul?" (Mark 8:36)

In 1999, that Bible verse came tumbling down when the grain elevator was demolished to make way for a highway interchange. So beloved and iconic was this building that the demolition created a traffic jam of viewers 2 kilometres long.

Pump It Out

Located on approximately 1.4 hectares of land on a single lot near Devon, Alberta, you will find an impressive piece of Edmonton's history. It's safe to say that this one landmark is what helped to make Edmonton the city it is today.

The Leduc No. 1 Discovery Well site marks the spot where the city first struck oil—and lots of it. When Leduc No. 1 first blew on February 13, 1947, Edmonton and area became known as the oil capital of Alberta.

After further exploration showed another rich resource under Alberta's surface—namely natural gas—new towns and businesses started popping up all around the Edmonton area.

Let's Make It Permanent

Concerned Edmontonians voiced their dismay and disgust when one of the most beloved buildings of their downtown core, the Canada Permanent Building, was about to become a strip club.

Public outcry began shortly after the City of Edmonton approved the plan for a gentlemen's club on two floors of the vacant historic building in September 2013. A month later, the proposal was dropped.

When the Canada Permanent Building was erected in 1910, it was built to last. This impressive testament to Edwardian baroque architecture still stands today, spread across two lots of land on 101 Avenue and 100 Street in downtown Edmonton.

When it was first unveiled over 100 years ago, the Canada Permanent Building was billed as Edmonton's first "fireproof bank." It was one of the first buildings in the city to have a structural skeleton made of reinforced concrete framing.

Alberta's Oldest Surviving Flour Mill

Just in case you're ever in the mood to search the province for its longest-standing flour mill, here's a good way to save time: just head to an office building on 101 Street and Saskatchewan Drive. These days, the Ritchie Mill is used by RE/MAX real estate and the Saorsa Business Centre, but when it was first built in 1892, it was a sign of the times. And the times were booming, especially if you were a farmer.

When Robert Ritchie first arrived in Edmonton in 1892 he saw a need for a flour mill in an urban setting. The development of the Strathcona community on the south side of the North Saskatchewan River also caught his eye. Putting the Ritchie Mill there was a no-brainer. Strathcona was where the train tracks ended.

Robert Ritchie would later serve in local politics as an alderman and, in 1906, as the mayor of Strathcona.

Holiest Place in the City?

Ripley's Believe It or Not once made Edmonton famous, especially among those who feel an attraction to all things holy. It listed Edmonton's 96 Street as the street with the most churches in the world (12, to be exact, many of them dating back to as early as 1909). The city's executive committee has been talking about giving the street historic recognition.

Whether or not people feel any kind of spiritual stirrings there is up to those who visit.

Odd Building

It's known by a number of names, including the Flatiron Building, the Gibson Block Building or simply "that wedge-shaped building." Located downtown on the corner of 96 Street and Jasper Avenue, the Gibson Block Building (its official moniker) is hard to miss.

Built in 1902 by William Gibson, this prototype of a flatiron building is known for its distinctive triangular shape. Its four-storey brick structure has seen an interesting history of businesses, everything from office and retail space to the much-talked-about Turkish Baths that closed in 1978.

Evicted from Government House

Located right next door to the Royal Alberta Museum is Government House, built in 1913 as the residence of Alberta's lieutenant-governor. In 1937, however, a disagreement between premier of Alberta, William Aberhart, and Lieutenant-Governor John C. Bowen resulted in Bowen's eviction. Following that, the building was leased by the U.S. army and the Canadian government. By 1951 it was being used as a hospital for war veterans.

In 1966, the Government of Alberta bought back Government House. Today, it has become a site for government meetings and conferences. The public, however, can tour the building on weekends and holiday Mondays.

The 100th birthday of Government House was celebrated in 2013, and it received quite the birthday present. It was declared a National Historic Site, making it the only structure in Edmonton to boast such an honour.

What a Square!

Here's a tidbit about the popular downtown square across from City Hall. Sir Winston Churchill Square was initially designed to be in the shape of Alberta—in an abstract sense, of course (since Alberta is actually more rectangular in shape). The middle of the square is meant to symbolize the prairies. The square's bleacher area is the foothills. The mountains are Three Bananas, a café on site.

As for City Hall, it sits, quite fittingly, at the top of the province.

Underground Hub of Activity

The Shaw Conference Centre is considered one of Edmonton's architectural marvels. At first glance, it's certainly beautiful. But it gets much more marvellous when you consider that its structure was built directly into the walls of the river valley. Designed by Edmonton architect B. James Wensley, the centre includes a glass atrium that cascades down Grierson Hill. Dig a little deeper and you'll discover that the vast majority of this 10-storey building is underground.

Achieving this feat of architecture wasn't easy. When abandoned coal-mine shafts were discovered on the site, construction costs went from $32 million to more than $80 million. The problem with mine shafts is that they collapse over time, making the ground unstable.

DID YOU KNOW?

In the early 1900s, a railway descended the hill where the Shaw Conference Centre is now. At the time, people had to ferry across the river and then transport horses, goods and *themselves* up the incline railway to the top of the hill. In tribute to that time period, the conference centre has an "incline escalator" and an "incline elevator." A particularly unique, even a little boggling, tidbit is that the elevators and escalators don't move up and down between floors but on an incline instead.

Artsy-looking

Never judge a book by its cover. In the case of the Art Gallery of Alberta, its spectacular outer appearance speaks volumes about the artifacts inside. Everything about this building screams art. There's a good reason why, in 2012, Randall Stout Architects was awarded the American Architecture Award for its design.

Opened in 2010 to replace the 1968 Edmonton Art Gallery, the Art Gallery of Alberta's curvilinear shape has more than injected visual flair into the downtown landscape. Crafted in patinated zinc, high performance glazing and stainless steel, the building is perfectly designed for the northern climate. For starters, its materials are extremely durable and also have a dynamic quality that allows the building itself to reflect the changes in light throughout the day and from season to season.

The building's interior is just as incredible. Boasting almost 8000 square metres, it is a premier presentation venue for international and Canadian art, education, scholarship and much more. There's a restaurant, a gallery shop, a 150-seat theatre, an outdoor sculpture court and even the fabulous "floating" Borealis Lounge. This private lounge doesn't actually float. It's simply a raised structure, but its glass walls do help to give the effect that you're suspended in the air.

With all of its artful newness, the Art Gallery of Alberta is the oldest cultural institution in Alberta, founded in 1924.

Endangered Power Plant

In the neighbourhood of Rossdale, located immediately south of the downtown core, sits a power plant that doesn't have power anymore. But it used to be a big deal.

Designed by award-winning architect Maxwell Dewar and built between 1931 and 1954, the Rossdale Power Plant represents the history of electrical power generation in Edmonton.

As the city grew, the power plant's structure was modified a total of six times over 22 years. The plant expanded each time, until finally it covered an area approximately the equivalent of two football fields. To say that this growth was controversial to the people who lived nearby would be putting it lightly. Over the years, some group or another always wanted it shut down. That only happened in 2008, upon the expiration of the utility company's operating licence for the facility.

The Rossdale Power Plant still stands—for how long is uncertain. It is the only remaining power plant of such size and age in the entire province, which is why it was designated as a Provincial Historic Resource in 2001. Heritage Canada lists it as one of the top 10 endangered historic sites in the country.

In August 2013, City of Edmonton councillors approved a move to save the plant, but that hasn't silenced the continued public outcry to have it demolished.

For the Love of Books (and Doughnuts)

Walk or drive along Saskatchewan Drive on the south side of the North Saskatchewan River and you will see an Edwardian-era red brick mansion that offers visitors a precious glimpse into Alberta's past. Built in 1895, the historic Rutherford House was home to Alberta's first premier, Alexander Cameron Rutherford, from 1911 to 1940. Rutherford had another claim to fame. He was the founder of the University of Alberta.

He was also a book lover—to the extreme. He once owned the largest collection of books in the entire city—approximately 3000. He had to hide the books around his house because his wife didn't want him buying anymore. To keep them out of sight from her ever-watchful eye, he even hid them in various nooks and crannies and under the beds of his children, Cecil and Hazel.

He did the same thing with doughnuts. Mrs. Rutherford didn't want him eating doughnuts because he was diabetic.

A religious woman, Mrs. Rutherford also did not approve of popular music. When their son Cecil got a phonograph, he tried to hide it as best he could. His mother found it all the same. But instead of throwing it away, she bought classical music to play on it.

In 1940, the Rutherford family sold the Rutherford House to a fraternity on campus called the Delta Upsilon. Two decades later, the University of Alberta planned to tear down the house and replace it with a new humanities building. The concept was successfully fought by the University Women's Club, which led the charge to raise the funds for its restoration—all $30,000 worth.

Rutherford House was designated as a provincial historic site in 1974, and today it can be rented out for private functions ranging from weddings to photo shoots. It is currently owned by the University of Alberta, which leases it to the provincial government for the cost of $1 per year.

DID YOU KNOW?

The University of Alberta was first established in 1908 with just 45 students and five faculty members. As a progressive learning institution, the university also helped in the valiant cause of women's rights. Its first president, Henry Marshall Tory, made sure that all courses and programs were open to women. The U of A's first female graduate was in 1912.

Suburban Mansion

One of these things is not like the others…

If you feel like scouting around, take a trip to the Gold Bar area of Edmonton, located at around 106 Avenue and 47 Street. The neighbourhood houses first appear to be little more than the typical modest bungalows from the 1950s and 1960s. But if you look closer, you'll see one glaring exception—a Victorian-style mansion sprawled across five acres of land. It even has an outdoor pool and a tennis court that backs onto the nearby ravine.

Care for a Drink?

Also in Edmonton's Gold Bar area is a weird little landmark that many people still refer to as "The Trough." You'll find it in a heavily wooded area of Gold Bar Park: a water well originally built for livestock back when the area was farmland. What you see today is a 7-centimetre pipe sticking out of the ground with gushing, fresh, clear potable drinking water. It runs all year, even in the middle of the winter.

It has been said that people in Gold Bar who make their own wine and beer collect the water from "The Trough" for its lack of chemicals.

The Rathole

On 109 Street between the avenues of 104 and 105 there used to exist an underground tunnel nicknamed the "Rathole." For many years, this dark and cramped tunnel was one of the most reviled components of the city's transportation network. For starters, it had only two lanes. In addition, visibility upon entrance and exit was hazardous. And it also was subject to flooding. Worst, some truck driver always seemed to miscalculate the height clearance of the tunnel and would get stuck there, causing a traffic jam at this major thoroughfare.

The Rathole was constructed in 1927 as a way for vehicles to drive beneath a span of 22 CN railroad tracks. Over the years, as many as 27,000 vehicles per day passed through it. By January 2000, the City of Edmonton—surely tired of hearing all the complaints about the darned thing—decided to demolish the Rathole and build a new six-lane divided roadway in its place, all at ground level.

The $5-million project was contracted out and completed in less than four months, three weeks ahead of schedule and just before the start of summer. In 2001, the contractor—the Toronto-based Morrison Hershfield, with an office in Edmonton—received the American Public Works Association Project of the Year Award for the assignment. It was the first Canadian project to ever win that award.

VISIT AND EXPLORE

Fort Edmonton Park

In 1895, H.G. Wells wrote *The Time Machine*, and to this day it is credited as the first book to introduce the daring concept of time travel. Ever since the 1960s, Edmonton has had its own form of time travel: Fort Edmonton Park. This fascinating theme park allows people to take a trip back in time.

Nestled in Edmonton's river valley, Fort Edmonton Park runs from east to west. In the east, the buildings, streets, displays and drama troupe members in period clothes are all dated in the 1920s. Travel westward and you go steadily back in time to 1846, when all that existed was a fur trading fort.

Along the way, you'll find certain milestones in the city's history. In the section of the park dedicated to the years 1885 to 1891, you'll witness the arrival of the railway. Along 1905 Street in the park, you will see how the advent of trains eventually made Edmonton more urban. The local economy may have been based mainly on agriculture, but the arrival of trains meant more professionals too. Suddenly, the city had practicing doctors and lawyers.

Fort Edmonton Park represents some other major milestones in its landmarks. You'll find a representation of the Blatchford Air Hangar, the city's first airplane hangar, opened in 1919. You'll also find a recreation of the Capitol Theatre, originally opened in 1918. Back then, it showed silent films to a capacity crowd of 150 people. In order to really sell the whole movie-going experience, the movies were advertised with elaborate 3D displays outside the box office. For example, a comedy called *Upstairs* had a 3D staircase leading nowhere, and *The U.P. Train* set up a complicated 3D train front.

Today, the Capitol Theatre in Fort Edmonton Park has three screens and is a 4-D theatre. You hear movies in surround sound and see them in 3-D. Some of the action also happens *off*screen. You can even *feel* some things.

What would H.G. Wells have to say about that?

Ukrainian Bookstore

The only Ukrainian bookstore in the city can be found in Fort Edmonton Park. It dates back to before the 1920s when thousands of Ukrainians started to migrate from farms to homes in rural areas. Soon enough, Ukrainian bookstores started opening up.

They sold more than books, however. The bookstores were also a great place to buy specialized food items such as *pysanky* (Ukrainian Easter eggs).

DID YOU KNOW?

Fort Edmonton has been moved a few times over the years. It was originally built by the Hudson's Bay Company on the North Saskatchewan River in 1795. In 1830, after severe flooding, it was rebuilt on higher ground near the present-day bowling greens at the Alberta Legislature building. Dismantled in 1915, a replica of Fort Edmonton can now be found in Fort Edmonton Park.

Fight for the Museum

The longstanding rivalry between Edmonton and Calgary flared up once again when museum director Ray Harrison said he felt strongly that Alberta's museum should be located in Edmonton. At the time, Calgary already had the Glenbow Museum, where some believed the "real" collections of the province resided. Because Edmonton was the capital of Alberta, however, the Provincial Museum of Alberta found its home right where Harrison wanted it.

Upon its inception in 1967, the museum took three years to build, at the cost of $5 million. It was later renamed the Royal Alberta Museum when the Queen of England paid a visit to the museum in 2005.

DID YOU KNOW?

When it comes to "real" collections, the Royal Alberta Museum is filled with them—and then some. Despite having a whopping 11 million artifacts in its collection, only one or two percent of the museum's full collection is on display.

Lights Galore

One of Edmonton's greatest holiday traditions is a trip to an eight-block stretch on 148 Street between 92 and 100 avenues. For two weeks each December, this otherwise entirely average area of over 140 houses is transformed by their owners into a world so magical that tens of thousands of visitors flock to see the lights of what has been dubbed Candy Cane Lane.

And what sights they are: life-sized nativity scenes, Santas, stunning snowmen, as well as Christmas stars, all blinking and beaming in full electric glory. Oh, and true to the namesake of the whole thing, you are sure to find more than a few monster-sized candy canes, too.

THE MAC

One of the most impressive buildings in downtown Edmonton is also one of its oldest. When it first opened in 1915, the Hotel Macdonald (simply "The Mac" to many Edmontonians) was named after Canada's first prime minister, Sir John A. Macdonald, to commemorate what would have been his 100th birthday. The Grand Trunk Railway built the hotel on the site of a former squatters' camp, which seems ironic considering that this high-end hotel was designed to serve the equally high-end passengers brought here by the country's expanding railway system.

Attention to Detail

Great attention was paid to detail in the construction of the Hotel Macdonald. Thankfully, a lot of those details are still seen to this day. All closet and bathroom doors in the hotel have the original Grand Trunk doorknobs—with the "GT" logo on them. The stylized initials on the doorknobs look like they say "CP," but they actually say "GT." As well, the woodwork in the lobby, the ceiling in the bathroom and in the Wedgwood Room are all original.

Perfect Wedding Place

Speaking of the Wedgwood Room, it used to be called the Palm Room, until it was redone in 1963. The renovations saw the room decorated with the official Wedgwood green and medallion shapes. It was due to the authenticity of the colours and the medallions that the hotel got the permission to officially call it the Wedgwood Room. Enter the room today and you'll see that it also has glorious round ceilings and a stunning Austrian crystal chandelier.

Saved From the Wrecking Ball

In 1953—during the massive oil boom caused by Leduc No. 1 six years earlier—hotel space was in great demand in Edmonton. To meet that demand, a 300-room extension or annex was built and connected to the Hotel Macdonald. It was so distinctly *not* artful that it quickly gained the nickname "The Box."

The Box was torn down in the early 1980s. Now in its place, just to the north of the hotel, is a beautiful park filled with flowers that are infinitely more pleasing to the eye.

The Hotel Macdonald itself was nearly torn down in the 1980s. The hotel had fallen into disrepair until its doors were finally closed between 1983 and 1991. It narrowly missed the wrecking ball until a City of Edmonton alderman named Terry Cavanaugh made the landmark's renovation his personal mission. In 1988 the City of Edmonton designated it a heritage building. In 1991, Canadian Pacific Hotels purchased it and returned the hotel to its original glory.

In 1999, it became known as the Fairmont Hotel Macdonald. To this day, it is one of the city's absolute must-sees. And to think that the hotel may have been simply turned to rubble!

DID YOU KNOW?

Melville Hayes, president of the Grand Trunk Pacific Railway, gave the go-ahead to build the Hotel Macdonald. Sadly, Mr. Hayes died before getting to see it completed—because he perished on the *Titanic* in 1911. A suite on the eighth floor is named after him: the Melville Hayes Suite.

Military Might

During World War II, the Hotel Macdonald was home to members of the U.S. military. They stayed in Edmonton while they were building the Alaska Highway—Highway 43, which connects Edmonton to Alberta's Peace Country and then on to Alaska.

After the Japanese attack on Pearl Harbor in December 1941, the United States government was in a hurry to build the Alaska Highway. It was intended as a link to northern airstrips, airports and radio ranging stations.

Construction of this 2700-kilometre roadway started in March 1942 and ended in October of that year, which is amazing when you think that much of the route crossed five mountain ranges. Apparently, if you need a big construction job done on time, call the U.S. military!

Royal Visits

Step into the truly luxurious Fairmont Hotel Macdonald and you'll see quite instantly why royalty stay there. The first royal visit to the hotel was back in 1919. The royal, in this case, was Edward, Prince of Wales (the king who later abdicated).

In June 1939, the Hotel Macdonald also hosted King George VI and Queen Elizabeth I.

In 1951, the Duke of Edinburgh stayed at the Hotel Macdonald with his wife, Princess Elizabeth (our current queen, Elizabeth II). The visit occurred just before she became queen.

Many years later, in 2005, Queen Elizabeth II stayed on the eighth floor of the Hotel Macdonald. Yes, that's right—she stayed on the entire eighth floor. Because the Queen of England is internationally protected, she had to have a whole floor, ensuring that no one in any adjacent rooms could harm her or spy on her. The whole affair was arranged when the general manager of the hotel received a call from the Canadian Protocol Office.

The largest suite in the hotel is named for the queen: the Queen Elizabeth II Suite. It is more than 220 square metres and is spread across two levels. The suite costs $3000 per night, and it is booked for approximately half the nights of the year—usually by newlyweds, celebrities and business people.

Providing accommodations for the Queen is, as you could imagine, quite an ordeal. In this case, the Royal Canadian Mounted Police (RCMP) and Scotland Yard took over the other rooms on the eighth floor and ran background checks on people in the hotel. In addition, the Queen's luggage had to be delivered by the Canadian military. Not a single piece of her baggage was handled by hotel bellmen or by any staff.

Preparing meals for the Queen proved to be an equally demanding task. The hotel chef cooked the lunch, and the restaurant manager became the official "Butler's butler," delivering the meals.

DID YOU KNOW?

It was during the 1939 visit of King George VI that Edmonton's "Kingsway" Avenue got its name. Technically, places named after royalty have to be officially visited by royalty. The same rule applies for the Queen Elizabeth II (QEII) Highway. Before the Queen's visit, it was simply called "Highway 2."

Monarchs and Movie Stars

Other monarchs who have stayed at the Fairmont Hotel Macdonald include a Japanese prince, the Netherlands royal family, the royal family of Thailand and the Prince of Monaco who, according to hotel staff, is an avid supporter of sports.

Celebrities and dignitaries have also stayed at the The Mac, and they include The Rolling Stones; Sir Paul McCartney; Sir Anthony Hopkins; Bill Clinton, who requested Cuban cigars; the Aga Khan (of the international Aga Khan Foundation, who came here when the University of Alberta gave him an honorary doctorate); Donny Osmond; and Leonard Cohen, who wrote his song "Sisters of Mercy" while staying at the hotel.

DID YOU KNOW?

When teen sensation Justin Bieber stayed at the Fairmont Hotel Macdonald in 2012, the park next to the hotel was packed with screaming girls. Hotel staff and management said you could hear them all the way down to the hotel basement.

WEIRD SCIENCE

Telus World of Science

In 1978, the Edmonton Space and Science Foundation was formed. Its goal was to build a science centre. But not just any science centre. This one was designed to look like a spaceship.

What is now officially called the "Telus World of Science–Edmonton" does indeed look out of this world. Its roof is slanted, for example, and that might make it look futuristic, but it's also for the usage of possible solar panels in the future.

True to its original design, the structure gives the illusion that it is floating. In part, this was helped by tinting all the windows black around the bottom of the building.

Something else is a little off-kilter about Telus World: originally, it was going to be built in Louise McKinney Park by what is now the Shaw Conference Centre. In its initial design created by famed Canadian architect Douglas Cardinal, the entrance for the science centre faced north. When the building site was changed to Coronation Park, the designs remained unchanged in regard to the location of the entrance—so today, finding the doorway is confusing for visitors.

The Edmonton Space Science Centre opened its doors on July 1, 1984. It became the first place in North America to have the largest domed theatre (named the Margaret Zeidler Star Theatre), an outdoor observatory and a planetarium. In March 2013, another first was scored when the science centre officials created a video link to the space shuttle, which allowed them to speak directly to astronaut Chris Hadfield in space.

ET, Go Home

In the late 1980s, a group of students from the Faculty of Engineering at the University of Alberta put a giant Reese's

Pieces on top of the Telus World of Science building. Although that may seem like little more than frat-boy hi-jinx now, it made perfect sense at the time. Back then, Hersey had an ad campaign depicting Reese's Pieces as UFOs. The students felt their giant mock candy made it look as though a UFO had landed on the building, considering it was a "space and science" centre.

Gross!

Sometimes science can get downright grotesque. That was the case with "Body World and the Cycle of Life," the exhibition at the Telus World of Science from May to October 2013. It featured more than 200 real human specimens preserved through an invention called "plastination" developed by pioneering anatomist Dr. Gunther von Hagens. These "plastinates" revealed, in intimate detail, the human body from fetal development through to old age, in health and in sickness.

DID YOU KNOW?

From 1995 to 2012, Edmonton's science centre used a ham radio station to link the science centre to the International Space Station. That same ham radio station was once used to rescue a couple from California who were lost at sea. The only people who picked up the couple's mayday were from Edmonton's one and only Telus World of Science.

Star Power

The Telus World of Science is known for its many displays and exhibitions devoted to science and fantastical thought. Fittingly, only two cities in North America won the bid for "Star Wars Identities: The Exhibition": Edmonton and Montréal.

Over the years, a number of out-of-this-world celebrities have landed at Telus World for one event or another:

- Mila Mulroney, wife of former prime minister Brian Mulroney, visited in 1992
- Jean Chrétien, former prime minister, helped perform various science demos in 2001
- Hollywood starlet Nicole Kidman and her country-singing hubby Keith Urban and their children visited Telus World in 2010

Other, less-known stars who fell into the orbit of the Telus World of Science include the following (exact dates of their visits are unknown):

- Shaun Cassidy, brother of 1970s heartthrob David Cassidy and star of the 1970s TV version of *The Hardy Boys' Mystery Hour*
- Norman Fell, who played Mr. Roper from that other 1970s show *Three's Company*
- Jeff Conway from the movie *Grease* and the popular 1970s TV sit-com *Taxi*, who was master of ceremonies for a fashion show held in the Margaret Zeidler Star Theatre

MEET IN MEAT TOWN

Meat Packing Capital of Canada

Until 1963, the Fort Road area in north Edmonton was called Fort Trail. More importantly, many people knew it by its nickname "Packing Town." The name originated back in 1908 because the district was full of meat-packing plants. It housed such major meat players as Swift, Burns, Canada Packers, and Gainers. From 1916 onward, it was considered the largest public stockyard in Canada. That title continued for almost the next 90 years.

During that time, Edmonton was considered the meat-packing capital of Canada. In 1916 alone, the area generated $4 million—a huge amount of money back then. Thousands of people were employed by Edmonton's meat-packing industry.

Patrick Dwyer, who owned a great deal of land in the Fort Road area, was the man responsible for bringing the first packing house—the Swift Packing Plant—to Edmonton in 1907.

DID YOU KNOW?

The Canada Packers meat-processing plant was constructed in 1935. That same year, it won an architectural award for its design. It surely should have. As the largest building of its kind, it stood a towering 10 storeys and cost $1 million to build—and at the height of the Great Depression!

What a Smokestack!

One of Fort Road's most noticeable and downright weird landmarks is the smokestack. Just north of Yellowhead Trail, the smokestack stands monolithically 30 metres high and is the last great remnant of the city's giant meat-processing industry. The smokestack served as the chimney for the Canada Packers power plant.

The rest of the building came down piece by piece in 1995. The smokestack, however, was given municipal historical designation in 2001, due largely to a big push by the Fort Road Business Association, which wanted to preserve it as a reminder of a meat-packing industry that employed so many people in northeast Edmonton.

The future for this unusual landmark remains to be seen. A new building will be built around the smokestack—a massive city-owned bus maintenance facility—but since the smokestack is protected by the City of Edmonton as a historical resource, it has to be kept. Part of the bid for the design was the stipulation that the smokestack be incorporated into the new building.

BEYOND THE CITY LIMITS

Jurassic Forest

The first thing you'll notice is the sound. It's an eerie, monstrous shrieking coming from inside the wooded area you're about to enter. For a moment, you hesitate. You think, "Do I really want to do this?"

Of course you do! Just taking that first step into the Jurassic Forest is the beginning of feeling like a kid again. And if you *are* a kid, try to pay attention to how your parents react. Study them closely as they round the corner of a wooden walkway and come upon a slight clearing in the woods only to be standing a few metres away from a triceratops…and it's *moving!*

With 51 animatronic dinosaurs in total (and counting), Jurassic Forest is the only dinosaur park of its kind in all of Canada, located a few kilometres northeast of Edmonton in Gibbons. It's the perfect setting for these moving, shrieking marvels of the prehistoric world. To see a *T. rex* or a family of raptors nestled in mysterious pockets of a green forest is nothing short of thrilling, whatever your age.

Jurassic Forest was created by a family from the Gibbons area in 2010. As they were putting it together over the course of two years, they somehow managed to keep this 40-acre park full of dinosaurs a secret. The secret was blown when the dinosaurs had to be moved into position by helicopter. Six weeks before the opening of Jurassic Forest, locals started talking after they saw the rather curious sight of helicopters carrying dinosaurs, and it wasn't long before the story ended up on the news.

Now that Jurassic Forest is up and running, its dinosaur stars are still freaking people out. Some of the visitors have actually asked, "Are the dinosaurs real?"

That might seem like the world's silliest question until you consider that moose also visit Jurassic Forest (real live ones, because they live and roam in the vicinity). The dinosaurs appear so lifelike that moose have attacked them—especially during the rutting season, when moose become more aggressive. The moose have knocked over raptors and have also snapped off a few dinosaur tails. The only deterrent is to put some wolf urine on the dinosaurs.

DID YOU KNOW?

A squirrel likes to hang out by the plaque in Jurassic Forest that includes information about what else…squirrels. (The little dude ran right across my path when I visited Jurassic Forest!)

Apparently, a number of visitors have asked whether the squirrel is real or animatronic like the dinosaurs. For the record, he's real. And very cute.

Prairie Gardens and Adventure Farm

It's a world unlike any other. Walk past the Lost Lemon Gem Mine, the Fudgery Junction and a small house shaped like a squash, and there's a good chance that the first thing you'll see is a little girl wearing luminescent fairy wings. Just a few feet away will be a boy dressed as a pirate. Then you start to notice something: almost all the little girls are dressed like fairies and almost all the boys have black eye patches, fake beards and pirate hats cocked askew.

It's all part of the Fairy Berry Festival, an event held every August long weekend at a 35-acre adventure farm located northeast of Edmonton in Bon Accord.

The Prairie Gardens and Adventure Farm is no average garden. It's a step into a magical place featuring sights such as a pheasant aviary, a petting farm and an enchanted forest that is honestly like a giant outdoor fort made by a kid. A really weird kid!

Kid can enjoy plenty of cool activities at Prairie Gardens too, such as three corn mazes, rubber duck races, tyke's tractor rides, and even a "corn cannon." In the fall, there's also a "pumpkin cannon." Have you ever seen an overripe pumpkin splat? You really should, at least once or 500 times in your life!

To keep the fun fresh, Prairie Gardens and Adventure Farm hosts oodles of different family-friendly festivals throughout the year, including a Corn Fest on Labour Day long weekend, the Fall-o-Ween Harvest every weekend in September, the Haunted Pumpkin Fest in October, and every spring they host a big Easter-egg hunt on the grounds.

Kubasa, Anyone?

Don't try to throw the interpretive guides at the Ukrainian Cultural Heritage Village off their game. To them, it's the late 1800s, and this massive open-air museum east of Edmonton is the real thing. The 30-something historic structures on site are their homes and their churches. All farming is done by hand—and by oxen, pulling what now seems to be antiquated, downright pre-historic farming machinery.

Families live in tiny houses, many of them with just one room. The beds are situated right by the stove, because it's the only way to stay warm in the brutalizing winter months. The eastern wall of one room is filled with religious icons. At the centre of the community is the church (mainly Ukrainian or Russian Orthodox churches with byzantine domes that make them look a little like mosques). The entrances of these churches face east. Why? Simple. Each day's sunrise in the east symbolizes the ascension of the human soul.

Spend a few hours at the Ukrainian Cultural Heritage Village and you will step back into much simpler times. You don't have to be eastern European to enjoy it. This village signifies what life was like for a lot of new Canadians who didn't speak English and had to make their way in a new land by working extremely hard.

DID YOU KNOW?

If you live in Edmonton, there's a good chance that either (a) your neighbour is Ukrainian, or (b) you're Ukrainian. Here's why. By 1930, a quarter of a million people from western Ukraine (Galicia and Bukovyna) had immigrated to Canada. There are over 250,000 Albertans of Ukrainian descent—the largest population of Ukrainian Canadians in western Canada.

Edmonton has the largest Ukrainian population in Canada, at 150,000.

Food Frenzy

I'm proud when I say that Edmonton is like a pair of sweatpants—not necessarily the height of glamour, but possibilities for growth are endless.

–Barbara North, comedian and co-host of *Press 2 Play* on Shaw TV

THE HISTORY OF YUM

Face it, everyone loves food. That's why there are so many food shows on TV (and entire food networks, for that matter).

Food lovers also love Edmonton—and with good reason. This city is home to an internationally award-winning chocolate, the perogy-flavoured potato chip and a great many ethnic restaurants: Lebanese, Vietnamese, Greek, Indian, among others. Numerous popular food chains also started up in our food-hungry city.

The love affair with food has been going on for a long time in Edmonton. Looking back in the city's history, you'll be perplexed to hear about some of the foods that were once considered the most beloved and trendy.

Like jellied salads.

The Great Grocery Famine

In 1883, back when Edmonton hadn't even reached town status, there was a grocery famine. It ended when the train finally arrived. On January 6, 1883, the *Edmonton Bulletin* ran an article about it, saying that "the train brought food but no bacon."

If you find it weird that bacon—or "no bacon"—could actually become a news item, remember: this is Canada, eh! Bacon has long been one of our signature foods.

The History of Beer

In 1887, the province of Alberta was still simply being referred to as the Northwest. Back in those pre-pioneer days, a law known throughout the land stated that you couldn't make beer *and* sell it. You could do one or the other, but not both.

A few years later, as if to show that civilization was truly starting to take shape, the South Edmonton Brewery opened in 1880. A quarter of a century later, in 1905, another brewery set up shop: the Edmonton Brewing and Malting Company.

By this time the law described above had changed. In over three years, the Edmonton Brewing and Malting Company produced over 20,000 barrels of beer.

Considering that Edmonton had only 8000 or so residents at the time, that's a lot of beer.

Hmm. Some things never change.

Show Off Your Pineapples

Back in the early days of the city, one of the ways a person showed they were well-to-do was by showing off their pineapples. That's strange but true. In the early 1900s, pineapples were rare in this part of the world. They were also very expensive. To own a pineapple, let alone serve it to your guests, was a sign of wealth.

For example, as the first premier of Alberta and founder of the University of Alberta, it would have been important for Mr. Alexander Cameron Rutherford to make a good impression on people of similar status. One of the methods for doing so was to ensure he had a home with at least a few jaw-dropping qualities. That was achieved, in part, by carving a pineapple design into the wood latticework at the entrance of the family's parlour.

There was a time when Edmonton was so frenzied over exotic fruit that people *rented* pineapples. It seems they just wanted to have them sitting in their house at parties, so they could look rich.

DID YOU KNOW?

Back in 1905, before the "pineapple frenzy," the advent of trains had introduced people to trendy new tastes. Popular food items of the time included anything that came in a can and anything that was jellied. Jellied carrots and jellied salads were particularly all the rage. One of the reasons why people bought iceboxes was so they could set Jell-O, in fact.

Fun Food Facts

If you're looking for trivia to share at a dinner party where there's that annoying lull in conversation, now you can impress everyone with your incredible knowledge of all things related to food in Edmonton:

- Edmonton had the first food bank in Canada. It was born shortly after a group of concerned citizens called the Edmonton Gleaners Association received their official charter of incorporation on January 16, 1981. If it seems weird that one of the richest provinces in the country would even need a food bank, perhaps it's better to focus on the positive: the Gleaners more than blazed a trail. Since that first food bank, more than 600 similar organizations popped up across Canada to provide food to those in need. The fastest growth in the number of people using Edmonton's food bank was between 1983 and 1984, but it was in 1996 that food bank usage peaked at an all-time high. The year of lowest food bank usage was in 2007.

- The oldest street vendor in Edmonton was a man known as The Popcorn Man. For 33 years, Sam Cherniak sold popcorn from a cart at 101 Street and 100 Avenue. He retired in 1971 at the age of 82. The Popcorn Man's cart still exists today. It can be found in the City of Edmonton's archive collection.

- The first official farmers' market in Edmonton was opened in 1900 by town council. It was located in the Churchill Square area for about 65 years, before being moved to 97 Street. It then moved to 104 Street downtown, where it is today.

THE SWEET STUFF

The Candy Man

In 2013, Edmonton's own "Candy Man" celebrated his 100th birthday. His real name is Bill McCreedy. There's a "sweet" story behind the nickname I've just bestowed upon him. On the cusp of the Great Depression in 1929—after working as a local newspaper carrier and one day before his 16th birthday—McCreedy started a new gig at the Pavey Candy Company.

His job was the kind you'd dream about having as a kid (or, hey, maybe as a grownup too). He used to make chocolates, jellies and caramels. Only eventually did he work up to hard candy, which was quite popular in those days, especially the black-and-white-striped "humbugs" that were Pavey's biggest seller.

The Pavey Candy Company also produced hard butterscotch, horehound twists, lemon slices and a weird little candy they introduced in the 1980s called "coal candy." Essentially, it was a hard candy made of black licorice, but it also looked like coal.

The idea was that you could use it at Christmas time, as a stocking stuffer.

Get it? Coal in your stocking?

As for the Candy Man, although Bill McCreedy retired in 1988 after making sweets with the same company for 59 years, he never stopped making candy. At Christmastime, family, friends, the banker and the family doctor all receive McCreedy's homemade treats.

Mmmm, Chocolate!

The man who brought Bernard Callebaut chocolates to Edmonton is also the man who invented "pre-washed" jeans. Although Edmonton entrepreneur Don Freeland is proud of revolutionizing the world of denim when he was vice president of merchandizing for GWG (Great Western Garment Co.), he considers Bernard Callebaut his single most interesting business venture.

On April Fool's Day 1985, Edmonton's first Bernard Callebaut chocolatier shop opened in the city's upscale 124 Street district. In its first week of opening, the chocolate shop raked in $5000 in just one day—with no advertising other than the canopy above the store and a promotional gimmick of delivering boxes of chocolates to nearby businesses in the area.

The magic ended in 2010 when fourth-generation, Belgium-born chocolate-maker Bernard Callebaut declared personal bankruptcy. When all the dust settled, Callebaut had lost the rights to his recipes and his Bernard Callebaut brand, but in 2012 he launched a new store called Papa Chocolat in Calgary.

Don Freeland and his son Michael, meanwhile, have a new chocolate shop in Edmonton's 124 Street area called Cococo. And they don't just sell chocolates. This distinctly European-style shop also offers delicious pastries, some of the tastiest espressos and Americanos in the city (or anywhere), and they make their own gelato.

Cococo offers new gelato flavours every week. Some of them are pretty experimental, like Curry Banana and Strawberry Cilantro. The latter was a mix suggested by a customer. In case you're wondering, it tastes incredible: sweet but smooth, with a distinctly refreshing aftertaste.

DID YOU KNOW?

Cococo entered in the prestigious International Chocolate Awards in 2012. Against some sweet competition from around the world, this Edmonton chocolatier won a silver for its Habanero Sea Salt, Thyme and Rosemary Milk Chocolate Bar. For a taste of it, ask for the "Rosemary Fusion Tablette."

On the off chance they have any left in stock, this sweet-and-salty chocolaty goodness will seriously blow your mind.

FAN FAVOURITES

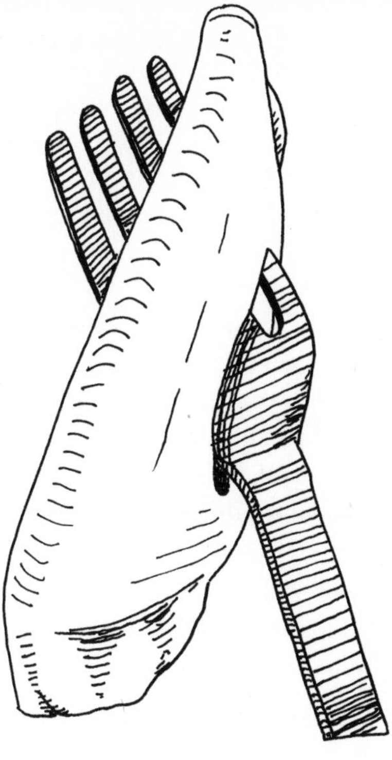

Perogy Power

Perogies are a doughy dumpling, usually stuffed with cheddar cheese, cottage cheese, potato or sauerkraut. Over the years, multiple flavours have been added—including blueberry. While most western Canadians know them as "perogies," their actual name is *pyrohy*. It's Ukrainian. Whether they're referred to as perogies or *pyrohy* doesn't matter. One way or the other, add some butter, sour cream and fried onions—and maybe bacon bits too—and they're delicious.

They're also popular.

In 1972, an Edmonton-based company called Cheemo decided to corner the market. Its founder Walter Makowecki started Heritage Frozen Foods Ltd. with the goal to provide consumers with high-quality perogies at a reasonable cost.

At first, the perogy-making operation was small, not much bigger than the standard one-car garage. To say that this family-owned business has grown would be putting it lightly. Heritage Frozen Foods now makes over three million perogies *per day*.

Perogy Potato Chips!

When Lay's Potato Chips put together a contest in 2013 to find four new flavours for their potato chips, the idea that came from Edmonton was a tasty no-brainer. It was called the "Perogy Platter." This perogy-flavoured potato chip was the inspiration of Lucas Crawford. He said it reminded him of home—as in Edmonton. And he's got a good point. Although we've never had a ton of Ukrainian restaurants, all you have to do is keep an eye out for a perogy supper happening at any local Ukrainian or Russian church. Or just visit a neighbour's house. They're probably having perogies for supper.

Sadly, Crawford's perogy-flavoured chips proved to have too regional an appeal. The winning flavour, announced in October 2013, was Maple Moose, created by Tyler LeFrense of Isle Aux Morts, Newfoundland. The chip flavour was released into the Canadian market the following month.

Green Onion Cakes

A popular ethnic food in Edmonton is, in essence, a salty, crispy pancake loaded with scallions. Add some hot sauce, and you have the recipe for an instant hit at any of Edmonton's many festivals. If you ask people, "What is your favourite food at the Fringe Theatre Festival in Old Strathcona?" the answer will probably be the same: "green onion cakes"—with a powerful dollop of sambal oelek (hot sauce) and soy sauce on the side.

Green onion cakes first became popular in Edmonton back in the 1980s. The first person who added them to his restaurant's menu was a man named Siu To, originally from Tsingtao in northwestern China. From there, word of mouth just grew and grew. Now, green onion cakes are served at almost every major summer event in the city.

Travel to restaurants in other cities and it will become fairly obvious that the green onion cake craze is something unique to Edmonton. Ask for them elsewhere and you might get little more than a puzzled look in response.

What the Truck?

In June 2011, a software developer and a food blogger teamed up to create one of Edmonton's tastiest festivals: What the Truck Food Festival.

If it seems like the world of software development and culinary delights don't go together—one of those ideas that makes you think, "What the…"—think again. As a fan of the ever-growing social media trend, Mack Male knew that there was also a growing interest in food trucks. His blog-writing partner Sharon Yeo felt the same way. Savvy to San Francisco's Off the Grid Fest, the duo wanted to try a similar food truck event in Edmonton.

Their festival started out in 2011 with seven food trucks and trailers. And it was a great success. Now the What the Truck Food Festival has "Big Events" of 10 or more food trucks three or four times a year. They're called "Truck Stops," and they're largely advertised through social media.

Fun on Wheels

The greatest thing about What the Truck Food Truck Festival is that the trucks seem to pop up in various neighbourhoods. And you never know exactly what sort of fun foods you'll get to enjoy.

Here are just a few examples of the taste sensations that you will definitely end up telling your friends about.

- The Carnival Cravings food truck offers mini-doughnuts with peanut butter, whipped cream and chocolate.
- The Bully Food Truck takes the whole peanut idea a little further yet. It offers peanut butter and bacon cookies. Yes, bacon (because this is Canada, eh!) One of the coolest things about the Bully Food Truck is that it gives a percentage of its profits to anti-bullying charities.
- The Lingnan's brand-new food truck offers some of the tastes that this 60-year-old Chinese restaurant is most famous for, such as its classic dry-and-spicy chicken.

DID YOU KNOW?

According to Mack Male, co-creator of the What the Truck Food Festival, Edmonton originally had a bylaw that said food trucks couldn't all be in one place. Due in part to the efforts of Mack and his partner Sharon, the City of Edmonton is now reviewing and changing these kinds of bylaws.

RESTAURANTS AND FAST FOOD JOINTS

The Oldest Restaurants

If you're in the mood to eat at a restaurant with a sense of history, why not check out the oldest restaurants of their kind in Edmonton?

- The longest existing restaurant in the city is a place that was called The Silk Hat, which was known for having gypsy-like tea leaf readers. The restaurant opened in 1913 and lasted until 2007. After that, this Jasper Avenue restaurant closed its doors, but then it was re-opened as a place where the hipsters hang out. It's now simply regarded as "The Hat."
- If your tastes lean a little closer to foods like stir-fried rice, gee gee chicken or crispy bo-bo pork, a trip to The Lingnan may be in order. (Yes, it's the same Lingnan that has recently invested in a food truck.) The restaurant's downtown location first opened in 1947, and some say it's the oldest existing Chinese restaurant in Edmonton. The Lingnan was also featured on the Food Network's Family Restaurant. As for "gee gee chicken" and "bo-bo pork," aren't those some of the coolest names for a meal?

Two Burger Kings?

These days, fast food outlets seem to be anywhere you look in Edmonton and many other cities. And there's fast food of all kinds now, including sushi. Back in the 1950s, however, the daily diets of Canadians didn't include doses of fast food. But that was soon about to change.

Here in Edmonton, the 1950s saw the rise of its first fast food place. Located on 112 Avenue just west of 82 Street, it was called Burger King, but it wasn't part of the famous "Burger King" chain of today. Eventually, this original Burger King in Edmonton lost the rights to the name, but as any kind of legal action goes, this one was slow. Edmonton's original Burger King had its name—illegally, really—all the way to 1995.

Round and Round We Go

It's not like the idea of a revolving restaurant is a new one. When La Ronde first opened in downtown Edmonton in 1967, however, it put a new "twist" on the notion of an eatery that spins. The uniqueness of La Ronde is its size; it's the largest revolving restaurant in the world, boasting a diameter of just over 30.6 metres. La Ronde is so large that it takes the restaurant one hour and 30 minutes to complete one whole revolution.

From its place at the top of a 307-room luxury hotel, La Ronde continues to provide its diners with an absolutely stunning view of Edmonton's magnificent river valley and the city's sparkling lights at night.

DID YOU KNOW?

The hotel that La Ronde is in—or *on*, depending on your point of view—is called the Chateau Lacombe. It's named after Father Albert Lacombe, a pioneer priest who played a significant role in the foundation of the province.

High-faluting Popcorn

Not far at all from La Ronde is the Fairmont Hotel Macdonald. Next time you're enjoying a drink or some food in either the Harvest Room or the Confederation Lounge inside The Mac, remember to make a special request: order some truffle oil on your popcorn. It's not on the menu, but it used to be. Some guests still remember it and order it. And now you will too!

A River Runs Through It

E-Town is full of people who are excellent at everything but bragging.

–Minister Faust, Edmonton author

ON LAND

Who knows exactly what happens in Edmonton's river valley when no one is looking? Maybe there's a Sasquatch that sets up camp, sipping tea from dainty china cups. Maybe there's a Swamp Thing–type creature lumbering about. And could there be an underwater monstrosity like the Loch Ness Monster slithering about at night? Or Ogopogo, at least? I mean, wasn't the latter reported to be found in Okanagan Lake in British Columbia? That's not really so far away, is it?

The fact is that there's a lot more to Edmonton's river valley than meets the eye. Amid this massive band of greenery and parks that runs through the city exists a whole lot of nature.

And as for Sasquatch, if you read the "Let's Go Wild" section of this book, you'll discover that some people think a sighting of that mythic creature just might be entirely plausible in these parts.

The sad truth is that a lot of long-time Edmontonians have never set foot in the city's river valley. They're too busy sifting through papers or spreadsheets under fluorescent lights at the office. Or going to the mall. Or sitting on the couch watching TV or playing video games.

In doing so, they're missing out on the wonder, the glory and the mystery that this river valley provides.

Green City

In a way, no city is greener—at least not on this continent. Edmonton's river valley features North America's largest expanse of urban parkland. This lush and peaceful green space encompasses the North Saskatchewan River and a whole series of major parks and nature areas—22 of them, in fact.

When David Byrne, singer of the 1980s "new wave" band Talking Heads, headlined the Edmonton Folk Music Festival in 2004, he raved to local media about the beauty of the city's river valley. It wasn't just because the folk festival happens in Gallagher Park, which is a patch of greenery in the river valley. Byrne also ventured out on the trails.

The river valley has 150 kilometres of walking trails, but they're made for more than walking. They're also used by many happy joggers, cyclists and, in winter, cross-country skiers and even people on snowshoes.

There is little doubt that Byrne, a New Yorker, would be impressed.

DID YOU KNOW?

The green space offered within Edmonton's river valley is 22 times larger than New York's famous Central Park.

The Perfect Segway

One of the best ways to see and experience the charms of the river valley is to do it on a Segway. If you've never heard of a Segway until now, they're a two-wheeled, self-balancing personal transportation vehicle. The actor Will Arnett was often seen riding one in the satirical TV comedy *Arrested Development*. The character that he played on that show—Gob Bluth—may have been an egocentric and almost completely brainless goofball, but take one short training session with the folks from Edmonton's River Valley Adventure Co. and you'll find out fast enough that SEGWAYS ARE COOL. (And, yes, that phrase is indeed deserving of ALL CAPS.)

River Valley Adventure Co. performs tours of Edmonton's river valley all year, even during the winter months, and you'd be surprised how many tourists are willing to brave the cold and see the river valley at its peak of frosty beauty.

How Do You Stop This Thing?

With almost a decade of experience under their belts, the trainers at River Valley Adventure Co. are considered to be the top Segway trainers in the country. Before you head out on your adventure through the river valley's many trails, the company's trainers will spend some quality time with you and your new Segway.

The most important skill to learn, however, is how to stop.

At first, riding on a Segway feels a little odd. It's a bit like hovering a few inches above ground at up to 20 kilometres per hour. Don't worry, though. Your Segway will be in the "beginner" setting, also known as the "turtle" setting, which doesn't exceed 13 kilometres per hour.

Here's the best part: it doesn't take long before you "get it," and when you start taking those sharp turns with confidence, you'll find a Segway is an incredibly fun way to tour the river valley.

The Star's Choice

Segway tours are a big hit with visiting celebrities. When English alternative rockers Muse played Rexall Place, they had a quick lesson on how to ride a Segway and then did some sightseeing.

The drummer from Taylor Swift's band did the same thing when the queen of pop country came to town in February 2013.

DID YOU KNOW?

Riding a Segway is good for the planet. Seriously. When you're using it to glide through Edmonton's river valley, you'll be producing absolutely no emissions of greenhouses gases. It does draw electric power to recharge, however. Still, that electricity produces 14 times less greenhouse gas emissions than your average North American car.

The Good Luck Lions

You'll see some interesting sights if you head through the trails on your Segway tour of the river valley. For example, you'll see two lion sculptures in Louise McKinney Riverfront Park. A gift from the People's Republic of China to the Edmonton Chinese Garden Society in 2007, the lions sit at the entrance to a serene Chinese garden that features a rather stunning gazebo that's open to the public.

The lion sculptures are also open for public use. In each of the mouths of those lions is a small, perfectly round ball of stone approximately four inches in diameter. Legend has it that if you reach into the lion's mouth and roll that stone around, you will receive good fortune.

Quite amazingly, each lion was carved from a single boulder more than 1.5 metres high. How did those balls get into the lion's mouths then? They weren't put there. They were carved that way—from that same boulder.

DID YOU KNOW?

Someone must have really needed some good fortune in October 2013. One of the balls from the mouths of the lion sculptures in Louise McKinney was stolen when the sculpture was vandalized. Repairs to the sculptures are slated for sometime in 2014.

ON AND UNDER WATER

Dragons in the River Valley

Something particularly cool happens in Edmonton's river valley every third week in August, rain or shine. The North Saskatchewan River comes alive with dragons. Well, it comes alive with dragon *boats.*

Edmonton's Dragon Boat Festival originated somewhere far, far away and an equally long, long time ago. Dragon boat races first took place in southern China more than 2000 years ago. Back then, boats adorned with dragon heads had a special meaning. They were part of a fertility rite. Putting a dragon head on your boat was seen as an effective way to ensure a season of sufficient rainfall and a substantial harvest.

That's not why dragon boat races are held worldwide to this day, however. There's a bigger story behind it all. It takes place around 277 BC, during which time there were warring states in China. In the State of Chu, a Chinese poet and diplomat named Qu Yuan rose to the office of advisor to King Huai. After the king's reign ended, Qu Yuan was banished to the rural area south of the

Changjiang River. During his exile, he wandered the countryside and influenced people through his poetry, criticizing what he deemed to be the corrupt powers of the day. When in 278 BC he heard that his beloved State of Chu had been taken by the neighbouring State of Qin, the grief-stricken poet allegedly put stones in his pockets and threw himself into the Mi Luo River.

As the legend goes, local fishermen raced out to rescue him. To scare away the mythic "water dragons" from Qu Yuan's body, the fishermen beat their drums. They also threw rice dumplings into the water, hoping the fish would prefer eating those to eating the beloved politician and poet.

Okay, it's morbid. But that's the legend. The tragic death of Qu Yuan is commemorated each year on the fifth day of the fifth lunar month, through the Dragon Boat Festival. Prior to this popular summer festival, local teams train to race their dragon boats down the North Saskatchewan River. Other teams take the race more seriously. They train to represent Canada in international dragon boat competitions.

Edmonton Queen(s)

Another great way to see the river valley is to take a ride on the *Edmonton Queen* riverboat. It first set sail in 1995. Since then, the boat has been a great source of entertainment and memory-making for everyone from wedding party members to corporate employees.

Speaking of entertainment—of an entirely different kind, that is—there is also a book called *Edmonton Queen*. It's not about the boat, though. Written by award-winning Edmonton playwright Darrin Hagin, the book documents the lives of the city's drag queens. It's more than a bit autobiographical. Hagin has performed many one-woman plays over the years. Well, they're actually one-drag-queen plays. (And he's a convincing gender bender.)

Fishin' in the Dark

While you're taking a leisurely cruise on the *Edmonton Queen* riverboat, look out at the water and you might find the odd fish. In fact, the North Saskatchewan River has no shortage of fish. Here are a few that you can fish for within the city limits:

- A river valley fish known as a burbot is recognizable by a single whisker that hangs from its lower jaw. It's also characterized by its dark body and white belly—and for its considerable size. It's a good 8.5 kilograms at its maximum weight. The longest known burbot was one metre.
- There are also five different species of suckers in the river. These fish are called suckers because of their thick lips that point downwards. They use them to suck food from the river bottom. And they must suck up a considerable amount of food. Suckers as big as 3.66 kilograms have been caught in the river. As for the names of those five different species, here they are: silver redhorse, shorthead redhorse, quillback, white sucker and the longnose sucker.
- As the largest member of the perch family, walleye are definitely big. The Alberta angling record for walleye is a weight of 6.7 kilograms and a length of 73.7 centimetres.
- But perhaps the biggest of "big fish" stories from the river valley has to be the lake sturgeon. They're easily recognizable by their long whiskers and the five rows of bony plates along their body. The largest fish in the river, they've been known to weigh as much as 47.7 kilograms and get as long as 1.7 metres.

DID YOU KNOW?

The lake sturgeon isn't just the biggest fish in the North Saskatchewan River. It's also the oldest. Many of them can live for over 100 years. As a species, they are far older than that.

According to the Royal Alberta Museum, the sturgeon is the living dinosaur of Alberta fish. It's part of a group of fish that dates back some 300 million years.

A Cautionary Fish Tale

According to guidelines set by Health Canada, you shouldn't eat fish caught from the North Saskatchewan River more often than once a week. Children under the age of 15 and pregnant women shouldn't eat the fish at all. And no one should eat the liver and other organs of any of these fish.

There's a good reason for this caution: the fish contain mercury. Humans eliminate mercury at a slow rate, and mercury poisoning can result in damage to the brain, kidneys and lungs. It can also lead to diseases such as Minamata disease, which doesn't sound like fun. Its symptoms include numbness in the hands and feet, general muscle weakness, and in the worst cases, insanity, paralysis, coma and death.

RIVER PEOPLE

Protectors of the River Valley

Simply said, the people involved with the River Valley Alliance are the sentinels of the North Saskatchewan River. The official mission of the Alliance is "to preserve, protect and enhance the river valley—to create one of the largest river valley parks in the world, and to create a legacy for generations to come."

The River Valley Alliance has an equally lofty vision: to connect the many parks, trails and other green spaces along the capital region into one continuous publicly accessible park. When that connection is complete, it will form the longest metropolitan park in North America (88 kilometres). It will also be one of the largest, with an expanse of 18,000 acres.

The Alliance was formed in 1996 by the seven municipalities bordering the Capital Region's North Saskatchewan River: Town of Devon, Parkland County, Leduc County, City of Edmonton, Strathcona County, Sturgeon County and City of Fort Saskatchewan.

When asked about what makes the river valley so great, Sol Rolingher, former chairman of the River Valley Alliance, said, "It is the heart and soul of Edmonton. It's the only thing in Edmonton that allows you to connect with nature—right in the middle of the city. It binds us together."

Even more poignantly, he said, "It's the best thing we've got."

A Home for the Homeless

Given the sheer size of the river valley, and given that it is so lush with trees, you can see why it's becoming a hotspot for the homeless. Boyle Street Community Services in the downtown core has a street outreach team that tracks the number of people it assists. It also tracks where they're located.

The numbers confirm that a great deal of people make their home in the river valley, whether that home is a tent or a cardboard box. From May 1 to July 31, 2013, the Boyle Street Community Service outreach team came in contact with more than 700 people living in the river valley. The year before, the number was 500.

In the spring of 2013, Edmonton police started using their Air One helicopter to spot "heat signatures" in the river valley in order to see where people were setting up camp.

DID YOU KNOW?

Edmonton's river valley is built on seams of coal.

The New Gold Rush?

Every year, droves of people still head to the North Saskatchewan River in order to spend their days shovelling gravel and breaking their backs while hunched over gold pans. They'll even gladly freeze their hands in cold October water. Why do they do it? They're searching for tiny particles of gold, of course. Mostly, though, these amateur prospectors are just in it for the fun.

During the gold rush of the 1800s, the activities of prospectors were not relegated to only the Klondike region of the Yukon in northwestern Canada. Prospectors used to sift through the North Saskatchewan River too, using gold pans, sluice boxes and even huge wooden dredges to collect gold from the river gravel.

NOTES ON SOURCES

The research for *Weird Edmonton* came from so many different sources, from books, from articles in magazines and on the web and from good old-fashioned face-to-face interviews with people.

For resource materials a writer can trust, I especially thank the *Edmonton Journal* and Old Strathcona's Tom Monto for accurate and interesting documentation about this fair city.

Some of the research for this book also came from the electronic world, and for that I thank Michael Gravel of MG Creative. He kindly set up the funky-looking Weirdyeg website that allowed me to solicit (and receive) great story ideas from the people out there in "cyber world." Twitter helped me spread the word about my research, but so did CBC Radio and Ryan Jesperson of *Breakfast TV* on City TV, who graciously invited me onto their airwaves to talk about all things "weird."

My deep appreciation goes to all the people I interviewed for this book, for being some of the most fascinating people I have ever met, especially the folks from EntitySeeker and Edmonton Paranormal Society. Regarding the latter two in particular, never before have I left an interview with my mind so completely blown apart (in a good way).

Here are some of the other people who graciously allowed me their time and access to their knowledge about a wide array of subjects for this book...

Barbara Smith, author of *Ghost Stories of Alberta* and many other fascinating books about the paranormal in the province.

Shirley Lowe, owner of incredible insights into the history of Edmonton's landmarks and in particular a deep knowledge of Old Strathcona.

Jack Morrow, whose unique brain seems to store everything there is to know about sports in Edmonton.

Mack D. Male, who is full of neat food facts.

Linda Hut of City of Edmonton's City Hall School, who introduced me to the "Poet of Churchill Square."

Yet others who provided great information for these pages include Donalda Pelton of Telus World of Science—Edmonton, Sally Scott and Suzette Mellado of Fort Edmonton Park, Deanna Fuhlendorf of the Fort Road Business Association, Tineke de Jong of the Old Strathcona Business Association, Bernie Borgeson of Edmonton Tourism, Kerry Mulholland of the Devonian Botanic Garden, Daryl Richel, wedding photographer Michel Feist of Ampersand Grey and the many others who are mentioned and referenced in this book.

ABOUT THE ILLUSTRATORS

Roger Garcia

Roger Garcia is a self-taught freelance illustrator based in Edmonton who works in acrylics, ink and digital media. His illustrations have been published in humour books, children's books, newspapers and educational material.

When Roger is not at home drawing, he can be seen facilitating cartooning workshops at various elementary schools, camps and local art events. Roger also enjoys participating with colleagues in art shows, painting murals in schools and public places.

Peter Tyler

Peter is a graduate of the Vancouver Film School Visual Art and Design, and Classical animation programs. Though his ultimate passion is in film-making, he is also intent on developing his draftsmanship and storytelling, with the aim of using those skills in future filmic misadventures.